If Singleness Is a Gift, What's the Return Policy?

Other Books by
MICHELLE McKINNEY HAMMOND

❧

What to Do Until Love Finds You
Secrets of an Irresistible Woman
If Men Are Like Buses Then How Do I Catch One?
The Unspoken Rules of Love
Why Do I Say "Yes" When I Need to Say "No"?
The Power of Femininity
Where Are You God?
Get a Love Life
Prayer Guide for the Brokenhearted
What Becomes of the Brokenhearted
Get Over It & On With It!
How to Be Blessed & Highly Favored
Wounded Hearts, Renewed Hope
Sassy, Single & Satisfied

If Singleness Is a Gift, What's the Return Policy?

HOLLY VIRDEN *with*

MICHELLE McKINNEY HAMMOND

THOMAS NELSON PUBLISHERS®
Nashville

A Division of Thomas Nelson, Inc.
www.ThomasNelson.com

Published in Nashville, Tennessee, by Thomas Nelson, Inc.

Authors are represented by the literary agency of Alive Communications, Inc., 7680 Goddard Street, Suite 200, Colorado Springs, CO 80920.

Scripture quotations noted NKJV are from THE NEW KING JAMES VERSION. Copyright © 1979, 1980, 1982, Thomas Nelson, Inc., Publishers.

Scripture quotations noted NCV are from THE HOLY BIBLE, NEW CENTURY VERSION, copyright © 1987, 1988, 1991 by Word Publishing, Dallas, Texas 75039. Used by permission.

Scripture quotations noted NASB are from the NEW AMERICAN STANDARD BIBLE®. Copyright © The Lockman Foundation 1960, 1962, 1963, 1968, 1971, 1972, 1973, 1975, 1977. Used by permission.

Scripture quotations noted NLT are from the *Holy Bible,* New Living Translation, copyright © 1996. Used by permission of Tyndale House Publishers, Inc., Wheaton, Illinois 60189. All rights reserved.

Scripture quotations noted NIV are from the HOLY BIBLE: NEW INTERNA-TIONAL VERSION®. Copyright © 1973, 1978, 1984 by International Bible Society. Used by permission of Zondervan Publishing House. All rights reserved.

Scripture quotations noted RSV are from the REVISED STANDARD VERSION of the Bible. Copyright © 1946, 1952, 1971, 1973 by the Division of Christian Education of the National Council of the Churches of Christ in the U.S.A. Used by permission.

Scripture quotations noted KJV are from the KING JAMES VERSION of the Bible.

Library of Congress Cataloging-in-Publication Data

Virden, Holly.
  If singleness is a gift, what's the return policy? / Holly Virden and Michelle McKinney Hammond.
    p. cm.
Includes bibliographical references.
  ISBN 0-7852-6329-2 (pbk.)
  1. Single women—Religious life. 2. Christian women—Religious life.
I. McKinney Hammond, Michelle, 1957– II. Title.
  BV4596.S5V57 2003
  248.8'432—dc21   2003006780

Printed in the United States of America
03 04 05 06 07 PHX 5 4

Contents

A Note to the Reader

To make it easier for you to know which author is speaking, Michelle's writing is set in san serif type to differentiate it from Holly's writing, which is set in serif type.

Introduction:
Here We Go Again!

Another singles book? Aren't there enough? How many times can we nurse and rehearse the same topic? I have to admit, I felt that I had paid my debt to single society with the four offerings for singles I wrote previously. As far as I was concerned, it was time to get over it and move on. After all, there had to be other things to talk about in life. Like where the hottest sale was, or how to spice up my home—anything but another round on how to survive singleness. However, when my friend Holly first mentioned the idea for a book called *If Singleness Is a Gift, What's the Return Policy?* I just hollered. I knew she was a nut, but this truly confirmed it. Of course, that's the reason I love her so much; she has such a wicked sense of humor.

Later, after pondering the proposed title, I thought, *Hmm . . . how appropriate.* I personally had resolved when I wrote my first book, *What to Do Until Love Finds You,* that I definitely did not have "the gift." But nine years have gone by, I've written many more books on the single life, and I'm still single and not any the worse for wear. Actually, I'm happier, which could be a good or a bad thing. Too much happiness can make you overlook something that might actually be good for you. It's called getting set in your ways. Perhaps I did have "the gift" and had failed to realize it all this time. Now if you had spoken to me ten years ago, I would have asked you to show me the counter where I could return the gift of singleness. But today I can safely say my singleness is a gift I have learned to treasure. I now consider a different type of return policy associated with the gift. Not how I can get *rid* of my singleness, but the returns I *receive* from my single status.

"What?" someone just shrieked. "What do I get out of being single? Absolutely nothing! Nothing but grief, snide remarks, cold and lonely nights, and increasing fears that if I ever do get married, I will have to resort to showing my new husband past photos of myself when I was smaller and saying, 'See, I used to be really cute.'" Not true! And you know it. You're probably getting better with age. You might not be a size 2 at this point, but your inner qualities should have blossomed to the point where your outer appearance is transformed by the fabulous woman you are as a whole.

There are returns from the single life if you use your free time wisely. Discover your gifts, and make the best use of them to chart a course for fulfilling your purpose and your destiny. Take the time to learn about yourself, who you are and who God created you to be, which will make you free to love, laugh, and thoroughly enjoy life as it is right now. Go to new places, do new things, discover new experiences. You are free to do it all. To eat from every tree in God's garden except one (you know which one I'm talking about—we'll discuss more about that later). Talk about your joy being full—I'm talking about having an interesting life because you can.

There is nothing and no one holding you back except your own excuses. So let's ponder this together . . . What do you get out of being single? Would God really leave us in such a state with nothing good to enjoy in the present? If God has chosen this time in our lives to be spent alone with Him, it has to be a blessing. A blessing that should enrich our lives and add no sorrow. Therefore, our singleness should be considered a good and perfect gift from the One who loves us most. It is up to us to see the value of it and learn how to enjoy it. Take it from two single sisters with a fifteen-year age difference, Holly and myself: There's a huge enjoyment factor in singleness. No, every day is not a picnic, but neither is every day of marriage. Married or single, we must learn to eat what is set before us and savor the flavor. Though Holly and I, both die-hard singles, can attest to the frustrations of living single and the desire for some things to be different, through this book we hope to give you inspiration to get the most out of your single journey and discover the hidden gifts along the way.

℮

With 79.5 million singles in the United States alone, I decided I couldn't be the only one wondering what the deal was. In my world, singleness is equivalent to leprosy; you've got it, and no one else wants it. Somewhere it was translated to mean there is something incredibly wrong with you, and marriage provides the only "cure." I wanted to figure this thing out, since it was becoming more and more apparent that it was my lot in life— temporarily, I hoped. The pressure to produce a mate to validate one's status in life can be overwhelming, yet Scripture is clear that singleness is a valid life choice, which means it's a valid life obligation to those of us holding out for the "I do's."

There have been way too many "You aren't married yet?" questions chipping away at my self-esteem, innumerable "What's wrong with me?" sessions turned into pity parties. My question some days really is: "If singleness is a gift, what's the return policy?" I have friends all over the country who also are floundering in their singleness. They despise every waking second of their status and live in a world of expectation and fantasy that may never even happen. When it does, disappointment is rampant. Most will camp at the park of loneliness and pine for a mate. Fewer will actually move on and discover that their present happiness is not dependent on their future. Do I think singleness is a gift? In it's own way, yes, absolutely. However, it's important to understand, that doesn't necessarily mean I want the gift forever!

I am certainly not above my own pining every now and then; however, Michelle and I, through our individual perspectives, want to pass along what we've learned and how we've resolved issues about our single status. It isn't as if we have all the answers, but we undoubtedly face or have faced the same dilemmas as many of you. I don't know about you, but I'm tired of suggestions, blind dates, and books with rules that want me to wait outside a men's rest room to find a date. I want to know what Christ would do . . . how He would handle it. Frankly, I want to know what is going on and why my number hasn't been called. After all, I've been standing in line for quite some time now. Just in case you're feeling the same way, know you're not alone— really! But the bigger thing to know is that there is joy right where you are. All it takes is a slight attitude adjustment, and you'll be on your way to having a much more fabulous life. So stick with us, and let's see what we can discover together.

1

If Life Stinks, It's Time to Change Your Perfume

Then Mary took a pound of very costly oil of spikenard, anointed the feet of Jesus, and wiped His feet with her hair. And the house was filled with the fragrance of the oil.

—JOHN 12:3 NKJV

Sweet scents. I can just imagine the fragrance of freshly cut grass in the spring, a misty day on the beach, or a fresh bouquet of flowers with its sweet scent wafting up. When the word *fragrance* comes to mind, what do you "smell"? I often think of my favorite perfume or that cologne my guy will wear. So often, smell dictates my emotions and triggers my memories. I don't know how you are about scents, but I personally was blessed with a stupendous sniffer. A particular aroma can take me back to a specific time and place and set me to dreaming about hundreds of scenarios of things I've already lived through.

While sitting in a college Bible class, the phrase "fragrance of singleness" was thrown out into the stagnant air of the classroom. This particular phrase threw my thoughts to the foul odor of old sneakers or a squished skunk. I felt that being single pretty much stunk. Being single pretty much stinks at some place and time for everyone. Everyone knows it! I am convinced that is why our married friends keep giving us all that horrible advice and keep setting us up on those atrocious blind dates month after pitiful month and year after pitiful year. If we were to investigate their actions of apparent malicious intent, we'd discover that it's just their way of caring. But I wish they'd stop. Oh, how I wish they would stop. But the reality is, they probably won't anytime soon because, after all, they care—and they know singleness does indeed stink!

Even without meddling friends or parents, our society is so couples-inundated, we have no safe haven. Many of us don't go to restaurants alone because we are afraid we'll be labeled a loser for dining by ourselves. The imaginary spotlight seems to follow us to the table where the sign pops up: "I'm alone because there is something wrong with me." Movies can sometimes be viewed in solo mode . . . but there is something about sitting all alone in a big theater full of couples.

Going it Alone

Speaking from personal experience, I know most single women break out in a cold sweat when it comes to buying tires or taking the car to the shop, largely due to the misconception that women are ignorant of such things. Men rarely need someone to go to the rest room with them, but they still prefer large groups at sporting events. Even if we choose the "safe" bet and stay home alone and watch TV, well, even there we have no respite. Popular television programs and commercials on any given night have more sexual innuendo than any one person needs to indulge in, in an entire lifetime, let alone thirty minutes. Couples are in, and singleness is out. It's been that way since the creation of time, though, so there's no sense in trying to change the vote of the masses. Adam was blessed with Eve because our Creator knew that it was not good for man to be alone. Unfortunately, my rib-providing man appears to be nowhere on the horizon. Sadly enough, I am reminded of that fact by friends and family constantly . . . as if I didn't notice the "missing party" already!

Coping with singleness is pretty much an everyday thing. We simply have to take it a day at a time. Personally, weddings are the most difficult for me. I was in college when my first "Pioneer Club" kid got married. Now keep in mind that many of my friends, significantly younger than me, had already made the trip down the aisle (as if that weren't dismal enough). But there is something especially depressing about the fact that a child to whom I taught Bible stories when she was barely out of diapers was now lapping me, a card-carrying member of the "single and looking" club. I had been actively hunting to win in the marital race for almost three-and-a-half years. I was in college, for crying out loud, with a mere three months remaining to finalize my "hunt" and obtain the much sought-after M.R.S. degree. There was pressure to perform, too! My father was (understandably) sick of providing for me. At that point he was so much more than willing to hand over the boat in the backyard for my betrothal fee. And then, of course, there is my dear, sweet mother, who means well and only wants me to be happy, but constantly chatters on about my being alone forever. Obviously, graduation from college came and went, but graduation into the ranks of the married was not a "degree" I earned.

Of course, you cope with the situation, deal with the loss of friends (they all pretty much disappear after they tie the knot), and you go on with your life, still searching for "the one." You're doing great, coping well, thankful that you don't have kids and can sleep till noon on Saturdays if you want—and then you get that wedding invitation from a "friend." You know the one. The one you *knew* would *never* get married, let alone *beat* you down the aisle. There is something about that moment that causes a cold chill to run up and down your spine. Mixed with disappointment, resentment, envy, anger—and yes, even a tiny bit of joy for your friend—you trudge to the local Hallmark to find a card to represent your "elation" (muttering under your breath). The perfect card for singles to send to those who cream us in the race would go something like this:

> Glad you found one
> I hope he measures up
> You know, of course, he is a son
> And his mother will drive you nuts.
> Happy Wedding Day

(I suppose there is a reason no one makes cards like that.) In our own selfish pain, we make a good showing and actually buy the mushiest card available because our prince or princess has yet to arrive on the scene, and we still have that imagery of grandeur.

We go to the ceremony (alone, mind you, because even our "backup" had a date), and deep down we really are happy for our friend. A little sad that it isn't us, but we know that once we find our mate, our match, we will be fine, we will finally be complete . . . someday. We rationalize that for every Jill there is a Jack, and surely they are wandering around out there somewhere waiting to be discovered. A friend of mine often states that her "Mr. Right" is obviously lost and won't stop for directions! Figures, huh? I'm assuming mine must be with hers!

After such thoughts settle back into the "place of dredged-up emotion," we revise our "They'll never beat us down the aisle"

4

list of people as we go. It's only after four or five times of trudging to wedding after wedding, seeing the people we have deemed "unmarketable" find their "true love," that we decide counseling might not be such a bad idea. It's upon the realization that we are sitting in our living room (with our twenty-something cats) living out the stereotypical old-maid role we never intended to play, that we slip into the depression of singleness.

REALITY CHECKS

There is a problem with our isolation and depression, though. While nearly all singles have bought into the idea that a spouse would complete them, no man or woman on earth can fulfill all our needs and desires. Oh, we know that in our mind, but try explaining that to us when we have a sunburn and can't quite reach our back to slather on the aloe. When we just can't get that bracelet fastened. Simply enough, we have our fantasy of marital perfection, and even though we know it won't be perfect, oh, it'd be so nice!

We aren't buffeted by the gloomy statistics of divorce because our relationship will be different; it won't apply to us. Then we start looking around at our married friends, family members, and neighbors and pick out things we would never do to our spouses. We comprehend and oftentimes bear witness to the fact that, unfortunately, the number of unhappy marriages seemingly far outweighs the number of happy ones, but we're sure it'll be different for us.

It's during those magical moments in ministry, when I see the Lord change hearts and lives right in front of my eyes, that I so badly want to be more like Mary (Luke 10:39–42) and consciously choose the better part. I have so many opportunities to utilize this season of life that fall through my hands because, sometimes, quite honestly, my pity party gets in the way. Deep down I know that I need to be active about His work, single-minded at the task. I have the "gift" (grumble and sneer), after all, but that doesn't lessen the pain of too many lonely days and longing for someone to hold me in the quiet hours of the dark night.

Trust me, I know the scenario! Sometimes we have been alone for what seems like forever, and we are desperate for someone to love and to love us back, and when someone shows up, well . . . at least they are here. I understand why people get to the proverbial "end of the singleness rope" and marry for companionship as opposed to love. You may be able to relate to the concept of "Well, they aren't so bad." But I want more for my life. Don't you want more for yours? It comes down to the fact that we have to truly want to experience God's best for us and choose to strive for nothing less.

I know it's not easy. But, I do know that His best for us is not you or me sitting in a house with a complete stranger, wondering what might have been. It is not us reading smutty romance novels or mindlessly watching soap operas, wishing the fantasy world that appears before us will soon be ours. I can also safely assume that God's best plan for our lives does not entail our sitting in a cold courtroom with a lawyer at our side fighting for us to get some kind of divorce settlement, because we couldn't handle the pressure of the man we had chosen to "settle for."

Nearly all of us have friends or family that find themselves single again (or you might be yourself), and they can tell us the cold, hard truth as no one else can. They have been there and done that and, sadly, if they had it to do over again, they would have made a better choice. They would have walked a different path.

CATCHING THE VISION

I think the key is to choose this minute to avoid situations that could develop into such scenarios—because there's too much to do, too many places to go, too much riding on what God needs to accomplish. We need to catch the vision of what our purpose really is. Being single can, of course, be hard, depressing, and even unpleasant at times, but there are so many incredible blessings and opportunities as well. We have to learn to see the glass as half full. I've discovered that while finding a helpmeet is important to me, it really is not the primary reason for my existence.

The biggest torment to me is that I regularly find Christian singles who occupy themselves with treasure hunts and bowling parties but rarely utilize their single status to turn the world upside down like those before us. How many Peters or Pauls or Marys and Marthas do you know? You know what I mean, the ones that really are on fire for Christ. These days, we run from activity to activity, which is supposed to count as our reasonable act of "service." I'm guilty of it, too . . . so don't assume I am just pointing my finger without the accusation bouncing back. But when push comes to shove, I want to be about His business! The road to hell is paved with good intentions, and how often do we assume our good intentions will somehow count for rewards in the end? At what point do we recklessly abandon our lives to His call?

So for those just stepping out into adulthood, and those who have chosen singleness on purpose, as well as those who have found it without looking for it, open your hearts and your minds to embrace Christ through it all. Because what I have learned is that the fragrance of singleness is not actually rotten sneakers. It's a bottle of perfume valued at a year's worth of wages poured out on the feet of Jesus. It's the love that surrounds us but so often gets displaced by our fast pace and overwhelming obligations. Although it appears to be a cross to bear, we *all* are called to pick up our cross and follow Christ daily . . . married or single.

The comfort in this is that the Lord promises that His yoke is easy, and His burden is light. So when singleness becomes too heavy to bear, reflect on the point that perhaps you are carrying a load not intended for you. Stop. Lay it down, and reach for the arms of the Lord. The pleasure of basking in the Lord's presence is indisputable. When you can do it with singleness of heart, the fragrance is sweet, and all the bitterness of life fades away.

℮

Holly, that's good stuff, but you know I have to throw in my two cents' worth. I recall jumping into a cab one day and the cab-driver saying to me, "Ooh! What is that perfume you're wearing? It is so wonderful! My goodness, I've never smelled anything like it!" I had to stop and think for a minute to remember what I was wearing, as I was in the habit of creatively combining perfumed creams with my spray fragrances. And if this combination had gotten such a reaction from a male, I definitely wanted to remember it and use it again. Such is life: Our attitudes become the fragrance that causes others to either be attracted or repelled by our presence. Gathering what we have on the shelf of our life and combining it to be a pleasing toilette that we wear with grace can make a huge difference as single women.

THE LOVER OF MY SOUL

When I first came to the Lord, I was excited, but not about being physically alone. I had to break off a relationship with a famous musician because he could not relate to my stand on celibacy or my excitement about Jesus at all. Because of my new love affair with the Lover of my soul, I had enough conviction and passion about what I believed to know that I was making the right decision to embrace my salvation and let Mr. Rock

Star go. However, when the fire cooled and I found myself alone trudging back and forth to church, dissatisfaction was birthed in my soul, and I began a trek that would last for a long time. I was miserable, and I made sure that everybody else knew it, too. I didn't have to say a word; it was all over my countenance. My life stunk, and I was disgusted with God. What happened to all the happiness I was supposed to be experiencing? Where were all the blessings I had been promised? I had been a good little Christian; shouldn't I get a husband out of the deal as a reward? Was this some sort of cruel joke? Oh, the injustice of it all! This salvation thing wasn't all it was cut out to be.

Praise God for His graciousness. He allowed me to fret and wrestle with myself until I was completely exhausted and then He gently said, "You know, Michelle, your unhappiness is your fault. You are bored with life because you have allowed yourself to become boring. Your attitude stinks. If anyone was interested in you, he would quickly change his mind if he got anywhere near you." The voice of the Holy Spirit sobered me and sent me dashing toward the nearest mirror to take a look at myself. What had become of me, the woman, since I had gotten saved? My life had changed drastically, but had it all been for the better?

We Go Through Changes

I thought about my habits and even my appearance. There were marked changes. In my attempt to look "holy," I had toned waaaaay down my flamboyant, though not revealing, manner of dressing. My routine had also changed. Gone were the art exhibits and other social events I used to attend. All I did was go to work, go to church, and go home. I didn't do this; I didn't do that. What was I trying to prove? All I had proved was that I was bored out of my mind! Salvation is a beautiful thing, but what we often do with it is not. In our fear of failing, and trying to prove to others around us that this great change has occurred within us, we go overboard. We throw out the baby with the bathwater. We stop doing all the things that made life interesting and joyful. We lose the part of ourselves that God wants to use. He needs all our different personality types to affect others for His kingdom.

This is not a release for you to go running back to a bar if that was your former habitat. All I'm saying is that Jesus said He came so we could have life and have it more abundantly. That means He should add more to our lives than we had going on before we met Him. Yes, some things should change, but our capacity to enjoy life should not. Life consists of more than work and church. There is a whole world of activity and various interests out there waiting to be experienced and cultivated. If we are salt, we need to be out there mixing and mingling, seasoning other people's lives with our presence and our witness. This interaction also keeps us razor-sharp and interesting as well as interested. Meeting new people, learning new things, discovering our purpose in life.

THE CURE FOR ONE-TREE-ITIS

I knew that I had graduated to another place the day I went to a wedding and was genuinely happy for the couple and didn't think, *I wonder when it's going to be my turn?* Instead, I thought, *Whenever, Lord. Meanwhile, I'm having a great time.* Wow! It was exhilarating to realize I no longer cared.

How did I get there? I stopped having "one-tree-itis." You know, that fatal disease that got Eve in trouble? She was so busy looking at the one tree she couldn't eat from, she forgot about all the other trees she *could* eat from. I decided to take as many bites out of life as I could. I took my life off hold and got busy traveling, taking various classes, entertaining friends in my home . . . As I started to move around, the conversations I had with people began to birth a burden in my heart for relational issues. Lots of people seemed to struggle with how to relate more intimately with God and with one another. God began giving me insights to share with others. Well, one thing led to another, and I ended up writing a book about it, and then another and another. Isn't that something? A natural progression from transforming a burden that was birthed through everyday interactions into my life purpose or mission. I have to admit, that is when full-tilt boogie-joy set in big-time, and I made an awesome discovery. The hole in my heart was not a person-sized hole; it was a purpose-sized void.

Not everyone reading this book was created to be an author/speaker type, but the bottom line is: You were created to do *something*. If you're not doing it, I can safely tell you that could be contributing to your state of dissatisfaction with the life you're presently living. I have to second the motion with God that if you're not happy, it's not His fault but your fault. He's already given you everything pertaining to life and godliness. It's up to you to use the gifts that He's made available, even take advantage of them to get what you want out of life. Chances are, if Mr. Right were to come along right now, even he could not make you happy, because you haven't located the true source of the joy factor for everyday living. So get busy, sister. If life stinks, it's time to change your perfume.

2 All Good Gifts Come in Small Packages

I wish everyone could get along without marrying, just as I do. But we are not all the same. God gives some the gift of marriage, and to others he gives the gift of singleness.

—1 Corinthians 7:7 nlt

As little girls, we are pointed to the day when we will find "the one," fall in love, and experience the grand "popping of the question." With the imagery of a diamond ring in a small velvet box, we've been dutifully trained to expect that all good gifts come in small packages. The last thing I got that came in a small package was an O-ring for my kitchen faucet, which blows that theory!

Since I'm a woman, the mere word *gift* generally causes me to smile. Who doesn't like gifts? That brings me to the gift of singleness. Isn't the "gift" just an "Oops, I forgot . . . Now what do I do?" type of gift wrapped in the comics section of the paper? Wouldn't it really just qualify as a "re-gift"? Something God had sitting around and wanted to get out of His house? Where is the "gift" in singleness? I haven't come to the conclusion yet that it is better for us *not* to be married than to be married. Have you? It can be a real cross to bear, and everyone knows it!

As much as I wanted to allow myself to daily sink farther into self-pity, I came to the end of me and realized the better choice was to figure this out—and quick—before I lost my calm, cool, collected mind! It was the apostle Paul who started the whole thing in 1 Corinthians 7. The chapter starts out discussing marriage, but Paul turns it into a commentary on why we should stay single. What does Paul mean when he says we should maintain the place in life to which the Lord has assigned and called us? Why does he say if we are unmarried, men should not look for a wife, and women shouldn't want a husband? Don't we have an option to be happy? I wasn't interested in Paul's rationale that it gave singles the opportunity to serve the Lord without interruption. I wanted to be interrupted. For years, I have been claiming Psalm 37:4 as my life verse . . . at least my *marital status* life verse: "Delight thyself also in the LORD; and he shall give thee the desires of thine heart" (KJV). (I should ask to see a show of hands of how many of you have "claimed" it, too!)

Well, a little background information seems in order. It was my desire to be married to a wonderful, godly man by the time I was twenty-three. Um, maybe I didn't pray loud enough. Okay . . . twenty-five will do then. My twenty-fifth birthday came and went, and I entered what I have come to refer to as the severe dating-drought time of my life. Unfortunately, there still isn't much "rain in the forecast." I was notably frustrated with the process—with God actually.

A Change of Plans

Since my parents accused me of being too "picky," I changed my "ideal man" list. I carved out all the sensitive, witty, funny, smart "desires" and knocked it down to the top two . . . male and Christian. I thought surely that would aid in the hunt. You know—open the margin for more potential. So I began my prayers with new fervor. "Okay, Lord, I'm giving You really good odds here. How about twenty-seven . . . twenty-eight . . . twenty-nine? Thirty, Lord! Can I please be married by thirty?" Please note that I have officially entered the thirties. I have a cat, I live alone, and will go on the record stating that I am everything I didn't want to be—namely, alone. As if that wasn't enough, my father is quick to point out that I am also adequately filling the real-life stereotypical role of an "old maid."

Time for a new approach, don't you think? "Okay. Hello, Lord! Do you recall the little shepherd boy turned powerful king, David himself, writing that if I 'delight myself in You,' then You will give me the desires of my heart? I have done the proverbial 'delighting' . . . *It's time to pay up!* And just in case You missed my previous fifty zillion petitions, my desire is to have someone to love and to be loved by!" To this He replied in my heart, "You already do." Knowing what He meant, and also knowing that He knew full well what I meant, I muttered on about all my sacrifices and my patience and my hope and my dreams and my timeline being off and how He knew I loved Him but I wanted a tangible person. Didn't He hear me? Didn't He care? "I have been very specific with You, Lord. I've laid it out for You. There is not a lot to be confused about here. After all, I've done my homework very well!" (Oh, of course the Lord and I play this little cat-and-mouse thing sometimes.) He replied, "When you pray, don't babble like the idolators, since they imagine they'll be heard for their many words" (Matt. 6:7). I didn't think it was very funny; however, I immediately resigned myself to review my "long-winded request" list.

Deciding that His will is, of course, sovereign and that it was fine to push my marital request back to another day and trust Him with an unspecified age, I decided to spend my morning studying His Word. I landed in 1 Corinthians 7. Needless to say, I didn't think that my "ordained" study was very funny, either.

> I wish everyone could get along without marrying, just as I do. But we are not all the same. God gives some the gift of marriage, and to others he gives *the gift of singleness*. Now I say to those who aren't married and to widows—it's better to stay unmarried, just as I am. (1 Cor. 7:7–8 NLT, emphasis added)

Now, I'd read this chapter dozens of times before. I suppose the real difference was, I was never in such a place of desperation before. As soon as I stopped reeling from what I construed as a sucker punch written out on the pages before me, my first reaction was to spout Scripture back to my Creator. "But Looooorrrrrddddddd!!!! (as whiney as you can possibly imagine!) You said, 'Whoso findeth a wife findeth *a good thing,* and obtaineth favor of the LORD" (Prov. 18:22 KJV, emphasis added).

After burying my head in dismay and disappointment, my heart finally returned to a normal beating pattern. With a deep breath and gulping down a considerable dose of my own pride, I prayed that He would help me figure this out. As obstinate as I felt at that moment, He was faithful to show me the bigger plan. The greater good wasn't necessarily marriage, but it didn't necessarily knock marriage out, either. Gee, what a deep revelation. I'm back at the beginning here, Lord!

GETTING A FRESH WIND

Stepping back to gain a fresh perspective, I attempted to conform my mind around the phrase "the gift of singleness." This book was titled that day, not out of disrespect, but out of sheer terror. "Lord, if singleness is a 'gift,' then what exactly is the return policy if we'd like to 'take it back'? I am even willing to take store credit from You!" As He gently led me back to His Word, the Holy Spirit comforted me, and visions of my destiny spent in loneliness and despair slowly subsided. I finally began to understand the "gift" of singleness as it relates to my life.

I was most pleased when I found that this call in 1 Corinthians 7 for the Christian not to marry wasn't a "directive" from the Lord. True, it was given by divine inspiration, but it was qualified as being simply drawn from Paul's own life experience. Paul himself said this was not a commandment; it was his opinion on the subject of marriage.

I don't believe that Paul was being a martyr or unrealistic in his offering here. Paul simply was able to grasp and wholeheartedly embrace the task of singleness of mind. He understood what it is to walk in Christ. For him, there was no question; his dedication was to the One who gave him life, and he chose not to divide his attention. He also understood and later qualified that everyone, in their own respect, has his or her own gifts from God. However, the gift does not necessarily have to be singleness; that was simply Paul's gift, and he knew its innate value.

The hardest thing about any "gift" is the suspense. The suspense with the gift of singleness is, basically, if I will ever get to trade it in for the gift of marriage. I tend to want to make frequent modifications to the plans God has for my life. I usually try to "approve" the path the Lord has for me, but that's not how He works. When He gives me an inch, I take a mile. I'm the one asking for a flashlight to see down the path, when He is only offering a lantern to see the next step. Paul had a grasp on what it meant to serve Christ. However, all too often I only have a grasp on what it is to serve myself.

A DAY AT A TIME

I'm still learning daily how to emulate Paul. To get to the point with not only my single condition, but with everything in my life, where I can say, "Not that I speak in respect of want: for I have learned, in whatsoever state I am, therewith to be content" (Phil. 4:11 KJV), and mean it sincerely.

When we stop to actually put it in perspective, you know, our little singleness "trauma" is hardly comparable to the four years Paul spent in prison. My blessed little life, filled with friends, family, a remote control to call my own, a dependable vehicle, and a home complete with central heat and air, is hardly anything to be discontented about. I am blessed beyond measure and find myself guilty of the worst crime . . . focusing on the one thing I am missing when my blessings are overflowing. I don't really want to hear about how my "tragedies" are minimal in comparison, but even at the worst, my life isn't worthy of being lived in discontent.

As a result of that realization, I've become what I refer to as a "Bottom Line" kind of gal with everything in my life. I worked as a financial analyst before delving into full-time Christian ministry, and in the financial world, the bottom line is everything. If it doesn't improve or negatively affect the bottom line then it just doesn't matter. End of story, period. Life is very similar to that. Jeremiah 29:11 (which is my "real" life verse) gives us the end of the story: "'For I know the plans I have for you,' declares the LORD, 'plans to prosper you and not to harm you, plans to give you hope and a future'" (NIV).

We read the end of the book first! So we know how the story ends: We win! It may not look like we thought it would look, but we *will have* a hope and a future. It may or may not include a mate on this earth, but it does involve a marriage on that side of the river. "I am jealous for you with the jealousy of God himself. For I promised you as a pure bride to one husband, Christ" (2 Cor. 11:2 NLT).

So, if my not finding a mate doesn't affect God's love for me (which it won't), and if it doesn't jeopardize my salvation (which it can't), and if it doesn't affect the outcome of my eternal destination (the bottom line), then it doesn't matter. The only thing keeping us from becoming content and closer to Christ is ourselves. Our frustrations, our thoughts, our self-focused, self-absorbed existence are the only things affecting the joy of the journey. Think about all the "gifts." From the gift of salvation to the gifts of the Spirit—all the way through to marriage and even singleness—all are still gifts. Think about this: "Every good and perfect gift is from above, coming down from the Father of the heavenly lights, who does not change like shifting shadows" (James 1:17 NIV).

Whether you land the gift of singleness forever or eventually trade it in for the gift of marriage, the key to enjoying whichever you presently own is simply recognizing the value. Whether or not you realize the significance of the gift you have will make a huge difference in how you treat it. If I handed you a brand-new diamond-inlaid Rolex watch, you would undoubtedly attach importance to it and take special precautions to protect it. But if I handed you a used Timex with a cracked face, which still kept perfect time, you would naturally hold that watch in lower esteem and would undoubtedly be more careless with it, even though a Timex watch "takes a lickin' and keeps on tickin'."

It's a given that the Rolex is a nicer, neater package, but it's designed to do exactly what the Timex does. What about you? How do you view your gifting? Are you doing what you were designed to do with the gift you now have, or are you still moping around, shopping for a nicer package? You don't have to think singleness is a great gift; it might be exactly like a used Timex to you, but it's what you do with the gift that counts. You can hide it in your drawer because it's embarrassing, or you can take advantage of its benefits. You can slap diamonds and gold on a watch, but it's still just a watch. In the same fashion, you can place frustration and disappointment on the gift of singleness . . . but it's still a gift. A good and perfect gift with worth and value, even if you can't see past the scratched surface.

℮~

Now see, you had to go there, didn't you, girl? You crunched on my toes a little, too, and I'm older than you. What you said brought back some painful memories of days when I used to be an opera singer. "Me, me, me . . ." in high C was my constant song—to an even worse melody. If I don't watch myself, it's easy to slip back to that place. We're all guilty. How I used to hate that Scripture: "Delight yourself in the LORD and he will give you the desires of your heart" (Ps. 37:4 NIV). Or how about this one? "Seek ye first the kingdom of God, and his right-eousness; and all these things shall be added unto you" (Matt. 6:33 KJV).

First of all, why did God have to be first? Wasn't it enough that we agreed to His terms for salvation? Didn't He know how difficult it was to live down here alone? Second, I doubted God's Word. I *had* been seeking the kingdom of God, so why wasn't He giving me what I wanted? Was there a time frame I didn't know about, like a civil service requirement or something? And last but not least, all my married friends would tell me: "Jesus is your husband, and believe me, He's better than a physical one." Well, that just made me want to hurt somebody.

I didn't want Jesus to be my husband; He wasn't here to dress up and go out to dinner with me.

EGG ON YOUR FACE

I have to warn you that God will listen to these types of conversations for only so long. The more you go on this way, the more egg you will have on your face when He finally answers you. Kind of like when Jonah was stuck in the belly of the whale, and the Bible says that on the third day, Jonah finally prayed. Trust me, "boyfriend" was praying looong before then. He just wasn't saying anything that God wanted to hear. I believe on the third day Jonah changed his prayer, and God said, "Now you're saying something, now we can talk, now you're acting like you have some sense!" Jonah got some sense all right; he had finally come to the conclusion that "those who cling to worthless idols forfeit the grace that could be theirs" (Jonah 2:8 NIV).

What exactly does that mean? Well, if I break it down I conclude it simply means that those who insist on life going the way they want it to miss out on the present joy and blessing, the present grace and mercy, that are available to them. You can put your life on hold and refuse to move until that man comes along—and get left out of the entire parade of life. In this case your desire for a mate has become a full-blown idol. And you know how God feels about that. He is not into sharing, so He will step back and allow you to become consumed with your desire. However, if you will pay attention to what He told the Israelites in Jeremiah 29:13, "You will seek me and find me when you seek me with all your heart" (NIV), some things will begin to change in your world.

Let me shed a little light on the situation in Jeremiah. The

Israelites had been led off into captivity in Babylon. Perhaps you feel as if you're held captive in your single situation, and you'd rather die than be a slave to loneliness. Well, God is saying that when you stop telling Him what will make you happy and just seek Him, He will show up and reveal a host of other options you can enjoy until He is ready to present the right person to you. Your pouting does not make Him hurry His agenda. He has promised to withhold no good thing from us. Therefore, this leads me to conclude that if it was good for me, I would have a man right now. If I am unhappy, it is because there is something I don't know.

The Heart of the Matter

We don't know that Jesus really loves us; it's head knowledge, not heart knowledge. We come to the Lord, and we learn that Jesus loved us enough to die for us, but I don't think we personalize the love of God beyond salvation. We don't fully grasp that this wonderful and Almighty God is interested in having a loving and intimate relationship with us. Therefore, we can't embrace the concept of God's being a husband to us as no earthly husband can be. We don't know or understand God's concept of what a husband should be, either. One who covers us, provides for us, protects us and loves us unconditionally. He is one who hears our heart, who is always open and available to us. Now that sounds good in theory, but it is a bill no human being can completely fill. Even after we have a physical husband, we will feel the need for something more—something more that only the Lord can provide.

As single women we must open our minds and hearts to a different concept of a "husband." Jesus really is your husband. As members of the body of Christ, we are collectively His bride.

We all share the same Fiancé. And believe me, Jesus is the only man who can handle millions of women and manage to make them all feel as if they are the only one! As you open yourself to the concept of having a divine Lover like no other, the Lord will open your eyes to see all the ways He provides for you, through miracles and supernatural favor as well as the kindness of others. He will have you feeling like a well-kept woman. He makes it well worth the wait until your natural husband arrives in the flesh. Because you are full of the love of the Lord, surrounded with His care, you are free and ready to have a healthy love relationship with your natural husband, because you will have more realistic and balanced expectations of him.

I put off buying a home for the longest time, holding out because that was the last thing I could leave for a man to contribute to my life (since I had already collected all my jewelry). However, after reaching the age of forty-five, I decided if I waited any longer I wouldn't have the energy to decorate or move anything, so I took the plunge. God showed up, led me to the right place, and moved mountains to get me a miraculous deal on a fabulous home. He didn't stop there; He had them throw in a bunch of upgrades and all the appliances for free! Now point to a man who could do better.

Can we talk about gifts here for a moment? No greater gift is there than this: that a man would lay down his life for someone like you and me. That man would be the Lord Jesus. But that was simply His first gift. We could see that He gives many gifts daily if we would only open our eyes. I think of Hannah in the book of 1 Samuel. She could have no children, and her husband had another wife who could. This made Hannah sad to the point that she couldn't eat, and her countenance was cast down. Her husband loved her so much that every time they went up to worship, he would give her a double portion for the sacrifice. But this didn't make Hannah feel any better. Finally, her husband said something very profound to her: "Why are you so downcast; why won't you eat? Doesn't my love mean more to you than ten sons?"

Hmm, doesn't God's love mean more to you than one man? It should, because He loves you, and He, too, has given you a double portion to make up for your lack in other areas. Have you taken note that you don't have to share your money with anyone? You can do whatever you please without consulting anyone else. You have double the time and space to do what you like as well. Take advantage of these free gifts—they won't last forever. They are precious gifts from your heavenly Fiancé. Act as if you appreciate them. This might sound like cold comfort to you, but trust me, there will come a day and a time when you will long for a late morning in bed, for a day when you can walk around scruffy and smelly and there's no one around to mind. This is the single's secret revenge—flaunt one of these experiences in the face of one of your married friends and suppress a secret giggle at the sight of their envy.

This secret I have learned: Jesus will be your husband. I'm famous for telling people I'm dating an old, rich Jewish man. Believe me when I say to you that He won't leave you out there on your own. He will walk with you as an able partner, ready and willing to assist you in every area of life. His ear is always open, and when you get still enough, you can actually feel and enjoy His presence. In moments like these, I can almost feel Him pressing a small and valuable gift into my hands that I can't wait to open. Could it be something from Tiffany's?

3 Singleness of Heart

*And they, continuing daily with one accord in the temple,
and breaking bread from house to house, did eat their meat
with gladness and singleness of heart, praising God, and
having favor with all the people.*

—ACTS 2:46–47 KJV

In his best-selling book *The Ragamuffin Gospel,* Brennan Manning
teaches, "We are made for the love of God, and nothing less will
ever satisfy us." This is truth displayed through words. Truth,
however, carries no weight if its authenticity is not empowered
through our actions. Unfortunately, our actions—or more accurately the lack thereof—regularly betray our heart condition
and our chronic lack of trust. Stop to think for a moment how
our lives would drastically change if we really internalized and
applied certainties such as Brennan's statement. What would
happen if we could truly grasp that nothing other than, nothing
less than, the love of God would satisfy our desperate yearnings?
How would contemporary Christianity change if we were to
come to that already established fact and truly embrace that

there is a void created by the Creator, for Himself to fill . . . alone. How would I be different if I took Him at His word and recklessly trusted John 15:9 in my heart? "As the Father has loved me, so have I loved you. Now remain in my love" (NIV). Better yet, how much joy could we bring to our King and residually to ourselves if we realized, as John Piper states in his work *Desiring God,* that "God is most glorified in us when we are most satisfied in Him"?

Singleness of heart isn't just something we as solitary adults need to grasp and implement into our lives. The directive is far-reaching and all-encompassing. I believe that singles, however, have the best opportunity to reach that position, pushing aside all obligations and seeking Christ with distinct singleness of heart. In theory alone, single people have less commotion and distraction surrounding their lives. However, truth be told, it is probably more realistic to assume that singles can become just as busy attempting to find value by investing their lives into married friends' families or taking on extra responsibilities at work or church and/or joining in other time-draining elective activities. Yet, notice that all these things could be justifiably set aside.

However, in spite of the differences or similarities found in the playing field between singles and couples, nearly all of us choose another way. Generally, it's our own way or at least our version of the way. I fear my big-screen debut in heaven showing my dedication to numerous things without any one commitment clearly defined. My busyness nullified by my lack of devotion. I've found the primary hurdle in my own life, of course, still revolves around myself. But let me be very clear—there are no exclusions to what the Lord desires from any of us. Every being in the universe needs to find his or her identity, individuality, value, and fulfillment solely in Christ and their intentional love for Him. No exceptions, no eliminations, no immunity.

Temporary Fillers

People most commonly try to surround themselves with friendships and other relationships to meet relational and emotional needs. Relationships, in the proper sense, are no doubt designed by God. It is apparent that He made us for one another because He saw early on that it was "not good for the man to be alone" (Gen. 2:18 NIV). Therefore, He has created us with an internal natural desire to have friends, acquaintances and, even more specifically, a mate. We were designed to have these relationships, healthily placed in our lives. Wouldn't you agree that God uses them to teach us the most? It is through interactions with others that we are able to reveal the delight of caring, the joy of encouraging, and the laying down of our lives.

However, something is still amiss in our world today. In this fallen humanity, more often than not we join with others not to give, but to get. We earnestly cling to one another, unknowingly conniving and manipulating the situation for our benefit. We are yearning for validity, something that ultimately makes your or my existence worthwhile. We are ultimately searching for an identity, an importance, a feeling of worth. All the while Christ stands at the door, knocking, holding our value in His nail-scarred hands.

These despondent cravings for any and everyone's acceptance and affirmation eventually permeate our lives and maliciously twist our source of self-image and worth. Soon our associations come to define us and our interaction with others instead of the Redeemer. The natural progression of things brings us to the fact that our "love" becomes conditional and temporary. When our needs are not met, the fondness turns to tolerance, and the quest for a new "friend" evolves. However, ironically, we as a society have yet to associate this with the current trend of divorce within our communities. Perhaps tuned out by our own uncertainties, we are only vaguely aware of the lavish number of unhappily married people around us. Individuals who undoubtedly walked into their marriage relationship armed with unrealistic expectations. We vow that we will not make those same mistakes, even though we do not understand what they are. Through careful examination, I've discovered that unrealistic expectations usually start out as hopes. Hopes, dreams, and desires that the companion who was meant for them is expected to somehow fulfill. The idea was that in one all-encompassing swoop of the hand, this union would indeed make them complete and fulfill the void that resides in them.

Based on how life plays out, that just isn't going to happen, nor is it a realistic burden to place on another. No man or woman, friend, lover, or helpmeet is able to fulfill all our wants, needs, requirements, demands, wishes, requests, or desires. In light of this, our unquenchable desire for marriage is gently pushed to the side and seen in a clearer perspective. Though the desire to marry is a healthy, God-given desire, we must understand that there is no human in the world who can fulfill us or take away spiritual emptiness. So why is it that we so desperately desire to be married? Because somewhere we were led to believe that a mate would provide all the missing pieces in our puzzled lives. Since that's not the case, we pause to wonder, *What will?*

FILLING THE VOID

Upon deeper inspection and exploration, I have come to hold the belief that our "God-shaped hole" is multilayered and multidimensional. It is deep and cavernous, unexplored and mysterious. Ultimately, it's unfathomable. Demanding that another human being carry the weight of filling it is neither rational nor just. That is like demanding that an ant dig a canyon. It is in the end an unrealistic expectation placed on someone who will not be able to complete the task.

Now that we have identified the problem, the solution may seem no closer, despite the fact that answers swirl around us. After all, we've come to depend on ourselves, so we trek farther into our own abilities. We may even come to understand that a companion would be unable to fulfill our fundamental requirements, so we establish our own system in an attempt to fill the gaping chasm, still looking and hoping that a mate might fit the bill as our desire to love and be loved lingers on. As I mentioned, we most often do this in our own strength and through our own means, which only serves to fuel the inappropriate response to our need.

We cling to the belief that we can actually make ourselves happy. We judiciously place planks over the void and function at a level we conceive to be normal. We resign ourselves to the idea that we will never be any happier than we are at this moment and bustle about to maintain the level we have achieved. Regularly, we spend our time sprinting about in the race of life buying things and collecting friends to fill the gulf between us and God. Spouseless people desperately hunt for a mate, still assuming that he or she will fill the "role." More often than not, we come up empty-handed, alone, and disappointed, still aching for answers.

As a society, we have come to focus on our circumstances, our shortcomings, and our misgivings, which sooner or later give way to an alternate reality we naively embrace. We struggle to keep up with it, unsure of the rules but willing to participate with the masses, as society tells us that right answers come in crowds. In other words, you're made to feel that you are wrong if you're not doing what everyone else is doing. It doesn't take long before we begin to whine. We cry that our finances are tight, our neighbors are crazy, our friends are too high-maintenance, our love life weak or nonexistent. All the while, the Lover of our soul is still standing off to the side, waiting for us to come to Him as He alone holds the healing balm, the missing piece of the puzzle, which for some reason we cannot discern will fit our hollowness perfectly. He is, in spite of everything, waiting patiently for us to realize that He alone can completely fill the empty space. However, whether it be pride, fear, or a myriad of other things, we simply avoid the truth, confident in our own ability to get the job done.

I know that avoiding the truth and depending on our own ability happens, because I've done it. I knew it happened to others when I sat next to a dear friend at lunch recently who a short time ago lost her precious husband. As we sat there discussing his passing and her heartbreaking hurt, the pain of her reality permeated our discussion. You see, her life had been so wonderful, yet it was lived vicariously through and was dependent on her husband. He was her protector, guide, spiritual leader, lover, and, in many ways, her savior. Her relationship with the Lord was noticeably second. Living it out, she and her spouse both loved the Lord and had a great marriage based on Christ, but in many ways, her "self" was in her husband. With him gone, she stands naked before the whole world with just her and the Lord to sort out her identity. Fortunately for her, she'll be just fine. She loves Christ wholeheartedly and is even now daily rebuilding her thought processes regarding the love of Christ. She's relearning to grasp that the love He has for her is more pure and more protective than even that of her precious husband. The void, exposed for what it truly was, is now being filled with His grace, mercy, and provision.

DEFINING MOMENTS

When we live in a situation where our identity is through our world as opposed to through Christ, what ultimately happens is that we become further desensitized to value. The world's value system is warped by comparison. It is based on how attractive you are, if you earn a six-figure salary, how large your home is, if you drive a foreign car, or if you are married, with children. When our relationships (or even the lack thereof) begin to define us, we are not controlled by Christ in us but by our own lusts and desires based on others' images and perceptions. In our efforts to fill the God-defined hole, we attach ourselves to things and others for the fulfillment of our relational needs. Ironically, there is nothing as consistently heartbreaking or less gratifying. We can, however, be free from the discouragement that is a result of these misplaced affections. We simply need to go back to the basic understanding that God is our source.

Catch sight of the fact that when this life ceases to exist, it's not going to matter what vehicle we drove, how nice our homes were, or how many friends we had. If for no other reason than this, I have learned that we must seek the Lord with a "defined" singleness of heart. We must obtain His affirmation and His acceptance and replace the props we have positioned in our lives, which only temporarily sustain our ever-slipping identity. We have to strip ourselves of the facades built on lies and mis-givings about our own value and worth fed by the world. We need to tear down our rickety fortresses and replace them with the stones of grace He offers to us. I don't care what your past looks like or what pillars you have created to fill your needs. I'm talking about a decision for today and for every today after. Please understand, the Lord loves us just the way we are, but He loves us so much that He is not willing to let you or me *stay* where we are. God is working in your life—even if you don't recognize it, understand it, or cooperate with it. However, sin-gleness of heart is not as difficult as it sounds to obtain or prac-tice. Simply enough, the point is to worship Him and love Him intentionally. He is worthy of our praise, worship, and love given with respect and sincerity.

Enjoying relationships and having friends and a mate to fill your needs isn't altogether a bad thing, but make sure the God-sized hole is filled by God and not those people you have surrounded yourself with. Our desires for friendship, passion, love, and intimacy are fashioned by Him for our pleasure and as a tool of training. Serve one another as Christ served, serving out of purity of heart rather than expectation of glory. If you can shift your heart and mind to capture the essence of God, you'll never want to please anyone but Him. Soon you will come to recognize all the pressures, cares, and concerns we have unnecessarily placed upon ourselves and the pitfalls we have avoided when we finally grasp that "we are made for the love of God, and nothing less will ever satisfy us."

I couldn't have said it better myself. However, this is a slow and painful lesson to learn. It usually sinks in after all your other idols have fallen or done you in. Bruised, battered, weary, and bowed, we come crawling back to the foot of the cross, where God gathers our crumpled spirit into His arms and does what He does best—comforts and restores. Why do we make Jesus the last resort? We treat Him like the nerdy guy who is always the last choice when we're selecting teammates in school. Yet we truly need His help to win the game of life.

LEARNING THE HARD WAY

Funny how we entrust our hearts into the hands of so many who are not qualified to hold them and then wonder why they drop them. Meanwhile, the One who has promised to keep our hearts safe rarely gets the time of day until someone else has broken what we should have given to Him in the first place. I suppose we all tend to learn our lessons the hard way, but is it really necessary?

Perhaps the problem is that God is good. And for the most part we find good men boring. We rely on drama for excitement. After all, it isn't really love without twists in the plot like we see on TV, is it? We would rather wonder, *What did he mean by that?* or *Why didn't he call me back when he said he would?* or *How many other promises has he broken? How many other lies has he told? Is he seeing someone else? What does that shift in his mood mean?* On the flip side there stands God, simply saying, "I love you."

Promises, Promises

Jesus is the epitome of the good guy. He doesn't look like Brad Pitt or Denzel Washington; He is merely easy on the eyes, no standout in a crowd, according to the prophet Isaiah. In His earthly body He didn't have any money or a top-notch wardrobe. He didn't even have an apartment! And yet He came seeking a relationship with us. That is still His heart's desire. What does He have to offer? He has pure intentions, He is forthright, patient, faithful, and consistent. He doesn't give up easily, but He doesn't push, either. And He simply cannot lie. There is none of the usual unhealthy drama we're used to having in our lives associated with having a relationship with Him. The drama all took place before. Seems kind of like a fairy tale. He pursued us, fought a dragon on our behalf, and has plans to return and carry us away to a fabulous mansion in the sky. To proudly present us to His Father and claim us as His own. After that, we will be served a feast to rival all feasts, far surpassing the most fabulous buffet you've ever attended, because it's taking them all this time to prepare it!

Wow! You might be rolling your eyes and thinking, *Promises, promises,* like that weary Samaritan woman at the well in John 4 who'd had so many men in her life who disappointed her, she wasn't able to recognize that she had finally met a man who could fulfill her deepest longings. We have allowed ourselves to become disillusioned by all the other failures in love we have accumulated. And yet in spite of us, Jesus, ever the good guy, says, "I stand at the door and knock. Why don't you let Me in?"

We at least give telemarketers the courtesy of listening to their spiel before we reject them. Do we give Jesus the opportunity to prove to us that He really can fill all those empty places in our hearts? That He really does collect our tears and is able to transform them into a soothing shower to wash away our pain and heartache? He is able to exchange beauty for ashes, weeping for joy, and fill our mouths with laughter and satisfaction. Oh, taste and see that God is good. But the only way you can do that is to open up . . . to realize that having singleness of heart is being focused on the wonderful surprises God will set before you each day as He enlarges your romantic territory.

4 I'm Fishing with a "Jerk Bait" Lure

fishing (noun) : a Jerk on one end of a line waiting for a Jerk on the other.

There is a new lure on the market that is catching so many fish, it is actually being banned from competitions. It's pretty amazing. The secret to the lure's success is that it is cut into four sections, which when pulled through the water imitate the actions of a real, live fish. Unaware fish think it's the "real thing," and apparently there are plenty that have been foolishly tricked into believing the illusion. However, just because it's not "real" doesn't mean it will stop me from using it on my family fishing trip. I figure if the fish is stupid enough to bite . . .

Ever pull out your best, most effective "bait" when you're fishing for a hunk or hottie? Fishing is different from dating, but not much. The same principles apply. There are different ponds, lakes, oceans, and rivers in which to troll. We take special care to pick out just the right "lure." To catch the "keepers" requires a little more work, and sometimes it's more trouble than it's worth.

Granted, in fishing the pond waters of dating, I do not have to deal with slippery worm goo or sharp hooks, but I do have to spend a little extra time in the bathroom polishing the "bait" with hairspray, makeup (a.k.a. "spackle"), and a wardrobe that tucks and hides my less flattering features (not to be construed as anything tent- or muu muu-like). Lighting provided at my destination enters into my decision making, much like the color sensor on what shade of shad you should use to fish when skies are overcast versus sunny. Actually, no difference at all really; I'm still casting out, giving the illusion that this is the "real" thing, and I do this even when I'm not sure what's below the waterline.

I think many singles make their mistakes right here topside. We trick the hunted (the opposite sex) into thinking that this is it . . . the "snazziest" thing out there. You can admit it—we *all* do it. When we start dating someone (or gee, even if we are just slightly interested), it becomes very much like the first week at a new job. We dress to make an impression. We become perky and accommodating and all of a sudden are efficient and cooperative. We smile (a lot) with our freshly bleached teeth and giggle at comments that really are bordering on lame. I even carry my lipstick and lip liner everywhere I go (trust me, this is not a normal occurrence for me). We do this because we want this someone to like us the same way we like them. We essentially start the game, letting them chase us until we can catch them . . . just like fishing for the big one. We don't want any "fish" to get away by jumping off the hook and slipping through a hole in our net, nor do we want "what might have been's" to permeate our minds if this relationship crashes. Oh, and we suspect that it will crash, because it's based on a whole lot of misinformation. We caught the wrong fish—in the wrong lake, at the wrong depth—because we were fishing with the wrong bait.

The Wrong Lake

I know Johnny Lee's country song with the line "looking for love in all the wrong places, looking for love in too many faces" is trite and overused, but since it still applies I feel the need to bring the twang to the table here. We dangle our bait in many different lakes. We fish in the oceans of the mall in high school, the lakes of nightclubs and bars in college (and after), then in the ponds of church activities, and with the onset of the twenty-first century, the Internet has become a popular hotbed of activity. The opportunities are unlimited. Different fishing spots have different "specialty fishes." Everyone knows you can't catch a shark in a lake—you have to go to the ocean. Too often we drop our line into the closest, easiest location that might produce a date, only to find the lagoon full of algae and dogfish—not a keeper in the bunch. To increase their chances of finding "the one," how many Christian people go to bars? Talk about catching the wrong fish!

The Wrong Depth

I love my fish finder. My brother got me a snazzy one; the fish show up with little pictures identifying their approximate size and location below the water's surface. These screens show you what is directly under the boat and at what depth the little fellers are hanging out. With any luck, by dropping your line to the depth at which they are "hanging around," you will be able to plan your next fish-and-chips dinner. There is still one little problem: You just are not sure what kind of fish it is. But there is always catch and release! My family gets irritated at me when I get bored with catching fish I never intended to land. Once I'm past a certain point, I throw my hook over the side of the boat just below the surface "to play." I watch all the fish come up to peck at my worm. I can entertain myself for hours doing that. (One of my lame ambitions is to take some of my cool lures to the quarry where I scuba dive and watch the fish's reaction first-hand as the lure jiggles through the water.) But the point I am actually trying to make is that fishing at the wrong depth will greatly impair your success! If you throw your line out in twenty feet of water but what you are trying to catch is at sixty feet, your chances of catching anything are slim, let alone someone you'd be willing to take home to meet your parents!

The Wrong Bait

Fish experts say every fish has some type of bait it "prefers." Sunfish and rock bass are keen on leeches and earthworms. Northern pike prefer chub or red-tail minnows on a Lindy Rig as well as Lazy Ike lures. Smallmouth and largemouth bass tend to be partial to Power Worms and Mister Twister Tails. Theory is, the larger the bait, the larger the fish. Now, it's not that I can't catch any other type of fish when I have those baits at the end of my line, but by choosing the appropriate bait, I am attempting to appeal to a specific type of fish. Despite my occasional fancy to "play," I am not an entertainment fisherman. When I fish, I want to catch a fish. More specifically, I want to catch a fish I can keep.

When it comes to the dating arena, too often I polish myself up to look like a "real" catch and cast out my best stuff, only to be disappointed when I recover what's at the end of my line. Is your social calendar filled with hit-or-miss dates that aren't any-thing close to what you're looking for? Just warm bodies filling an empty slot or saving you from a perilous evening at home alone? What about your wardrobe? Are you dressing up your bait by wearing clothing that suggests you want something contrary to what you are truly looking for? Are you doing and saying things that attract the opposite of what you really want? How many of us have countless numbers of married friends who pull out the now notorious line: "Well, I wasn't looking [for my husband-to-be]! It just happened!" We outwardly roll our eyes, inwardly claim that we aren't looking, either, and still wonder if her new husband has a decent brother. Sound familiar? There has to be some logic in the madness. Jim Schettler, my college pastor, issued a dating challenge to me years ago, which I think is lock, stock, and barrel better than our current plan. It's pretty easy: *Don't look for the right one. Be the right one, and you'll find the right one.* What should our plan be? Let's break it down.

Don't Look for the Right One

I bet you're wondering where I learned all the fishing language spouted above. To shed some light on that, you have to understand, I come from a fishing family. My mother's parents started the trend, and from the time I was born we faithfully went on annual family fishing trips to Brainerd, Minnesota. We still go every so often (as a family), and it's still one of the best vacations I take. When I go, I don't wear makeup, comb my hair too much, or paint my nails. I look quite the fisherman in my flannel shirt split open to reveal my long underwear and my fillet knife sticking out of my belt loop. But I don't care; I'm dressing for the fish, and the more "rotten" I look, the more I catch!

On one of these vacations, I was about six years old and my brother was two. Picture if you will two kids, two adults, and one rowboat with a 9.6 horsepower outboard motor on the back.

The time is past sunset, approximately nine or ten at night. The sky is boasting a clear Minnesota night, a sliver of a new moon, and a crisp, flowing breeze gliding across the glossy, glasslike lake.

My dad had heard at the bait shop that our lake was producing some great catches of walleyes. The bad news was, the "hole" was located at the farthest point away from our cabin, on the other end of this massive lake. So, it was on this particular evening my parents decided to try the rumored spot. Due to the fact that this noteworthy species of fish was mostly obtainable only when it was dark, we navigated our seasoned boating crew to the northeast late into the evening.

We arrived at the site after what seemed like forever and bunkered down for a night of fishing. We cast out our lines and trolled, essentially unsuccessful for a couple of hours. Well past boredom and with the fatigue of the day creeping up on this six-year-old, I snuggled down on the floor to join my brother and await our journey home. When the wind started picking up, my parents decided we'd better head back to our cabin, which, if you recall, was on the other side of the lake. Truth be told, it was probably only five or six miles, but it seemed like a hundred. The wind steadily picked up, producing some whitecap wave action we were forced to endure. Waves came crashing against our tiny boat, spraying us with chilled water, and the cool breeze whistled through our wet jackets. Wet, tired, and cold, I hunkered deeper into the life-jacket-based bed we had created.

We were about halfway back when the engine began to sputter. It was only a matter of seconds before it made its final lunge and came to its ultimate stopping place. My brother and I were snuggled up, still lying in the hull of the boat watching the stars "zoom" by to pass the time. Once the engine stopped, Mom whispered for us to stay put and not move. We lay in the silence and listened to Dad try to restart the piece of equipment with no result. Pull after pull after pull. He was silently hoping for any kind of spin from the prop to get us home, but to no avail. After a few choice words, it was settled; we had run out of gas. In view of the fact that Dad was the one who'd thought half a tank of gas would be enough, Mom awarded him the primary slot of chief rower for the newly formed "scull" team.

Dad had been rowing diligently for quite a while at this point. We knew this because he had to change seats, and now his back was to us as he tried to propel the boat toward the bright light marking our origin. I had been staring at the same star for an extremely long period of time. I knew he was rowing, but I wasn't sure if we were moving or not, so I decided to check it out for myself. The wind still howling over my ears, and the waves still spraying my face, I stood up as the boat wobbled a bit under my stumbling six-year-old effort. I strained to see the shoreline and where our nice, warm, cozy cabin was waiting for us. My eyes landed the destination, and a frown grew on my face because the target was still so seemingly far away. My pondering ceased when a growl from my irritated father erupted from behind me: "Lie down! You're wind drag!"

I wonder how often the Lord wants to say that to me. He's got it all under control, yet I want to stick my head out and poke around for some direction to see if I can offer some measly assistance. I'm trying to locate the "goods," and I'm just slowing Him down in what He's trying to accomplish in my journey. He's got the timing all in place, and I'm trying to detour, and head the way I think is best.

Stop trying to find "the one." Christ already has your life mapped out. He already has any future mate for you all selected and is working even now to get you both ready at the predetermined time. It's apparent to me that each man is awarded the task of finding his wife. Adam did the hunting and God did the providing. So women, lay low, and call off the manhunt. Men, be diligently attentive to your task. It also seems clear that your role as believer is to allow God to shape you into the person He wants you to be for your mate. My tiny, self-fulfilling contribution still involves my praying for *whom* I will marry, not *if* I will marry.

However, when we do finally find each other, He will have created each of us to be what we need to be for the other. Stay out of the way, stop the restless searching for a mate—Lie down, you're wind drag!

BE THE RIGHT ONE

This entire book is dedicated to the foundation of "being the right one." I need not drag out what you have already read or will read. However, be careful not to miss the simplicity in the truth that we attract what we are. Have you had a string of high-maintenance or selfish dates? Better check to see what you are portraying. If you're living out a life that screams, "I will do whatever I want, whenever I want," you are choosing a life contrary to what God teaches and will likely attract the same. The implications of your actions could prove to be detrimental to your life, since all your decisions are based on the myopic view of "I."

Biblically speaking, the best advice I can give you is to live out your life according to Romans 12:1–2: "Present your bodies a living sacrifice, holy, acceptable to God, which is your reasonable service. And do not be conformed to this world, but be transformed by the renewing of your mind, that you may prove what is that good and acceptable and perfect will of God" (NKJV). Put it into practice using the guidelines set in this verse. Carry yourself as a child of God, a new creature renewed in Christ. Proverbs 3:6 says, "In all your ways acknowledge Him, and He shall direct your paths" (NKJV).

You'll Find the Right One

There is no lone correct formula for finding "the one." I'm not offering a guarantee with this theory, but rather trusting in the sovereignty and faithfulness of God. If you are walking with the King, in the control of His will, you are still bound by His timing. No amount of cajoling or begging will bring about the right one outside His plan. There is no law of averages based on the number of dates that will increase your odds of finding "perfection." However, I know that if you have the desire to be married, God has more than likely placed that desire in you and, according to His Word, we should inquire of Him.

> Ask, and it will be given to you; seek, and you will find; knock, and it will be opened to you. For everyone who asks receives, and he who seeks finds, and to him who knocks it will be opened. Or what man is there among you who, if his son asks for bread, will give him a stone? Or if he asks for a fish, will he give him a serpent? (Matt. 7:7–10 NKJV)

While this isn't a surefire guarantee that we'll find a mate, we know that God's character is displayed in His Word. If we take Him exclusively at His written promises to us, we can cling to such verses as Matthew 7:7–10 and others:

> LORD, thou hast heard the desire of the humble: thou wilt prepare their heart, thou wilt cause thine ear to hear. (Ps. 10:17 KJV)

> Thou hast given him his heart's desire, and hast not withholden the request of his lips. (Ps. 21:2 KJV)

> The Lord is not slack concerning his promise, as some men count slackness. (2 Peter 3:9 KJV)

> He who finds a wife finds what is good and receives favor from the LORD. (Prov. 18:22 NIV)

Stand faithful as He works in you, and pray His Word. Abandon yourself to His will and stop using "baits" and "lures" to catch just anything that comes along. You have been called to receive more as a child of His kingdom and to be "confident of this very thing, that He who has begun a good work in you will complete it until the day of Jesus Christ" (Phil. 1:6 NKJV). In light of this, be faithful to lean on His knowledge and provision, and trust Him to bring you the right one in the right time.

❧

I just looove the fishing analogy; it rings so true. Unfortunately, I think too many single women have misinterpreted Jesus' words about being "fishers of men." He meant men's *souls*, ladies. Their souls! Anyway, I recall an experience I had on a fly-fishing trip. Ever since I saw Brad Pitt in *A River Runs Through It* I had wanted to try it just once, so when a dear friend of mine, who was also my publishing guru, said he wanted to take me, I dashed off to acquire blue jeans and sneakers for the occasion. Whenever I mentioned the upcoming fishing trip to my friends they doubled over in laughter at the thought, but I was ready to go.

The day came and we got into a little sailboat and coasted down the most gorgeous river in Oregon I had ever seen. Bill explained to me that it was the off-season or something like that. I'm not as knowledgeable on this as you, Miss Holly. All I know is the bottom line was I would have to throw back whatever I caught because the fish were all babies and needed time to mature for the real fishing season. That seemed reasonable to me; this was all about the adventure.

Well, there we sat. Bill baited my hook for me, as I was not touching anybody's worms even if they were God's creations. He then showed me how to cast (that means throw the line out), and I was hopeful it would land somewhere good. Then we just waited. It was not advisable to manipulate the line or wiggle it to catch attention. Just be still and wait . . . Hmm . . . Finally, I felt this little tug on my line. I got so excited I jumped and started jerking on the line and pulling it in, only to find that my catch had escaped. I had assisted the fish in slipping off the hook with all my premature yanking. I learned quickly to wait until I was sure it had been hooked before trying to pull it in.

After finally mastering this technique of waiting, I caught several cute little fish, all of which Bill gently removed from my hook and threw back into the water. He laughed because I winced at their pain and was afraid to touch them lest I do greater harm to them while trying to let them off the hook. Yet I had the time of my life catching them. He concluded I was sadistic as I said, "Poor little fish; let's catch another one."

The Waiting Game

Are you getting where I'm going with this? The fisherman is in pursuit of the fish, yet he or she must wait. "Wait on the Lord" . . . that has to be one of the most excruciating Scriptures in the Bible. How powerless we feel. You mean I should just sit here? Shouldn't I be doing something? Well, yes, you can enjoy the scenery. As I sat there in that boat, I sometimes almost missed the yank on my line, so absorbed was I in the beauty that surrounded me. Never had the sky been more blue, the mountains more majestic. Truly God is an incredible artist, and I know Him personally. What a privilege to know One who is so awesomely creative. Yes, enjoy the scenery of life. Look at all God has made available to you, and revel in it.

I think of the Lord when I think of how Bill put the bait on my hook. I don't think we have to manipulate anything about ourselves to catch the attention of the man God has for us. God Himself will place something in us that is bait for that man. There will be something about me in his eyes that draws him to me, muttering under his breath, "Bone of my bone, flesh of my flesh."

Now here's the tricky part. When he approaches for a nibble don't get excited, you could lose him. Just be cool. Though the man is the one who should be doing the pursuing, a woman must know how to keep him on the line. Wait until he has bitten off enough to be hooked. In other words, don't commit your heart, mind, or body too early and scare him away. Just be still, wait on the Lord, and wait until that man is committed to hanging on. Then gently draw him in. The dance of romance changes hands many times, creating tension and release. In actuality a woman catches her man by allowing herself to be caught. Now remember, I caught many fish that day, but it was not the proper season. The fish were not mature enough to take home. I couldn't get rid of them myself, but Bill gently did the work for me.

KNOWING YOUR SEASON

Be cognizant of the season. You need to be able to determine if the man in your life is mature enough for the role he will have to play. You will attract many, but only one will be for you. Don't take it personally, just leave them where you found them. Allow God to gently remove them from your life, and continue to enjoy the journey. Don't get upset, lose your balance, and tip over the boat. If you do, the fishing trip will be over as the fish scatter and head for safer waters. You will only end up cold and wet. No, stay centered in the safety of the Savior's care for you, and keep sailing.

How interesting it is that the line must be cast away from yourself, cast into the deep to even find those fish that live beneath the surface of what your eye can see. God always calls us to stretch beyond our comfort zone, where we presently are, in affairs of the heart. Faith says that even though you cannot see him, he is there, waiting, hungry and expectant that soon he will happen upon some delectable morsel that will catch his eye and satisfy his inner longing. And then one day he sees you just sitting there, looking tasty . . . you turn slowly and smile. Then reel him in.

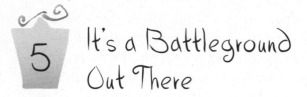

5 It's a Battleground Out There

With him is an arm of flesh; but with us is the LORD our God to help us, and to fight our battles.

—2 CHRONICLES 32:8 KJV

Since I spend half my life traveling aboard planes, I have more stories about travel than you'd care to hear. I usually can't tell them to my travel mates simply because it would be kind of like watching the movie *Titanic* on your cruise vacation, if you catch my drift. So please indulge me for this flying story:

On a commuter flight from Portland, Maine, to Boston in 1987, the pilot heard an unusual noise near the rear of the plane. The captain, Henry Dempsey, turned the controls over to the copilot and went back to investigate. As he reached the tail section, the plane hit an air pocket, and Dempsey was tossed against the rear door. He quickly discovered the source of the mysterious noise. The rear door had been improperly latched prior to takeoff, and it flew open. As a result Dempsey was instantly sucked out of the tiny jet.

The copilot saw the red light that indicated an open door. He radioed the nearest airport, requesting permission for an emergency landing. He reported that the pilot had fallen out of the plane and asked a helicopter to search the area. After the plane landed, the ground crew found Dempsey holding on to the outdoor ladder of the aircraft. Somehow he had caught the ladder and held on for ten minutes as the plane flew 200 mph at an altitude of 4,000 feet, and then, when landing, he kept his head from hitting the runway, which was only 12 inches away. According to the news reports, it took airport personnel several minutes to pry Dempsey's fingers free from the ladder.

In an effort to save himself, Henry Dempsey clung desperately to the only thing that could rescue him, and his grasp had become locked into place.

GET A GRIP

What is your grip on Jesus? How tightly do you cling to Him? Do you have a loose grip on the Savior, knowing He'll always be around to clean up your mess, or are you clinging to Him desperately because He's your mainstay? If you are hoping to stay single forever, to find the man or woman of your dreams, or even to avoid the person of your nightmares . . . regardless of which camp you fall in, there will undoubtedly be battles along the way! We get so used to being assaulted by a variety of things—the opinions of others, fear of the future, financial struggles, the clanging of the biological clock, the weariness of going it alone

. . . Shall I go on? Where is the balance between being still and bailing or fighting? Your grip on God can make all the difference. It's a given that war paint, combat boots, and heavy artillery wouldn't be a bad idea, either! (Guys can still wear battle fatigues and pull it off with gusto. However, girls, in an effort to appear more feminine and more socially acceptable, we can just carry our pepper spray!)

Nevertheless, regardless of your physical gear, spiritual preparation, or what direction your journey takes you, the confrontation cannot be ignored. The key is what you choose right now—how you're going to fight. When push comes to shove you have to know what you are going to cling to, because fight we will, on one plane or the other (no pun intended). "For we wrestle not against flesh and blood, but against principalities, against powers, against the rulers of the darkness of this world, against spiritual wickedness in high places" (Eph. 6:12 KJV).

What better place to discover how to thwart and get through conflict effectively than in a historical account of both figurative and literal theaters of war, all ripe with lessons! It's so advantageous to find strategies that have both won and lost campaigns, played out by a wide array of characters in the Word of God. We can learn from the first king of Israel, Saul, who spent most of his early life and subsequent kingship focusing on his circumstances instead of concentrating on the task at hand. His son, Jonathan, despite the desolate circumstances, forged ahead in obedience to God. Saul camped out under the pomegranate tree, counting his troops, and Jonathan acted on what he did know (that they had been given the job of defeating the Philistines), and he was *not* paralyzed by what he did not know (that the outcome was unsure in light of the large variance in army size). We see Jonathan's faith in action and Saul's tragic lack of it. Can you identify with Saul, who was regularly paralyzed by what he *didn't* know and was generally overwhelmed by what he *did?* Or are you more of a Jonathan, bucking the odds even when they look grim because you know the battle isn't really yours but God's?

Then there is David. The psalms are full of his successes and failures. David was called a man after God's own heart, in spite of all his very public falls. What made the difference between Saul's failures and David's? Saul fell and wallowed. David fell and followed. David's grip on Jesus was tight. He wouldn't let go, whereas we have to wonder if Saul had his hand near God at all.

What about Ruth's grip? Scripture records her saying to her mother-in-law:

> Entreat me not to leave you, or to turn back from following after you; for wherever you go, I will go; and wherever you lodge, I will lodge; your people shall be my people, and your God, my God. Where you die, I will die, and there will I be buried. The LORD do so to me, and more also, if anything but death parts you and me. (Ruth 1:16–17 NKJV)

She forsook everything she knew in her life to follow the path of bitter Naomi. Fortunately for Ruth, the King of kings had paved a way for her. Her good choices, strong character, faithfulness, and tight grip on Jesus were eventually rewarded through God's provision of Boaz, her husband.

STEP OUT IN FAITH

What about Solomon, Samson, Peter, and Judas? What characteristics made or broke each of them? Solomon, the wisest man who ever lived, reigned forty years and then turned his back on the Lord in the last minutes of the game. He almost blew it as his wives turned his devotion to other gods and idols in the land, but he was saved by his dad's name . . . King David. Samson, a Nazarite who was set apart from birth, defeated a thousand men with the jawbone of a donkey (Judg. 15:15), but was tragically deceived by the lust of a woman time and again, culminating in his premature death. Peter was faithful and then faithless, all within a few moments. Walking and sinking, praising and denying. Judas, oh, deception filled Judas. Talk about one man you wouldn't want to be. He was obviously one of those guys who had half the luck to have been chosen to be part of the inner circle and half the brains not to use his role effectively.

However, who among us can point fingers? I find myself judging Saul as if he's the only one who's ever been guilty of lacking trust. Unfortunately, I can often respond exactly like Saul. I roll my eyes at Solomon and Samson, both who had a weakness for the ladies, but I buy into some pretty stupid things myself. I sure can't stand back with my arms crossed, tapping my toe and judging them, when I pull similar shenanigans at times.

Peter—oh, my, do I ever feel for the guy. I probably feel so sorry for him because I'm just like him. I'm all fired up, but too often my grip on Christ is only as tight as my faith is in the moment. Toss in chaos or trauma, and all of a sudden my grip loosens and my eyes grow wide. It may be a Peter scenario where we are called to get out of the boat for a move, a job change, or to endure this world as a solo warrior, but we sometimes prefer to hold on to sinking ships. Most times we can't see through to the other side of the situation; therefore, our trust is questionable. We are called, equipped, expected, but still lacking faith to make it happen. How often do you find yourself in that predicament?

Sometimes we'll take the first step or two, defying the circumstances, but then somewhere along the line we look around at how impossible it seems, and we begin to sink, just like Peter.

We grow complacent in our comfortable place where we justify and rationalize that it is better to wrestle with the known enemies of today than the unknown of tomorrow. We stretch ideas and thoughts to try to make sense of the happenings in our life and understand why certain things occur over others. Really, truth be told, we are too limited in our vantage point to comprehend God's purpose, as were Saul, Solomon, Samson, Peter, Judas, and a slew of others. The bottom line is this: Either you will have faith working in your life, or you will have doubt working in your life. Which will it be? The ones who repeatedly fell had one main problem: They lacked the constancy of purpose that is key to success and greatness.

There are some examples that display the constancy of purpose, the even keel we desperately need to master: warriors like Joseph, Job, Hannah, Hosea, and Paul. I encourage you to dive into their stories and discover the details of why they survived the battles of life. They weathered the storms clinging to the King. How many times have the proverbial "what-if's" prevented you or me from taking on a task that we knew we were supposed to undertake? Are you fighting with God or against Him? Is there some self-imposed deadline that you are waging a war against? Are you fighting with yourself over your single status? Are you like many in that the fear of being alone sometimes overtakes you, and the doubts begin to creep in? All of a sudden you grasp the thought that maybe you *had* the right one at some point but missed him because you were too wrapped up in Mr. Right Here.

Battles are inevitable, and as often as I fight against the battle rather than with it, I am reminded of Romans 5:3–5:

> Not only so, but we also rejoice in our sufferings, because we know that suffering produces perseverance; persever-

ance, character; and character, hope. And hope does not disappoint us, because God has poured out his love into our hearts by the Holy Spirit, whom he has given us. (NIV)

Our actions (or once again the lack thereof) will reveal where strength or weakness lies.

I recently heard the saying "If I had the power of God, I would change my circumstances. If I had the wisdom of God, I wouldn't." *Smack! Pow! Whap!* Holy Batman, that hurt! How many times would that be true if we saw the whole picture, knew what He knew? What lessons do we unknowingly forfeit? Would any of us make it through what Job endured with his attitude? "Though He slay me, yet will I trust Him" (Job 13:15 NKJV). How brave we think we are when we make decisions based on what we know will happen, but He's calling us to get out of the boat and walk on water in faith . . . to simply trust and obey.

It doesn't matter what the fight is, whether it's life in general or something outside our control. Undoubtedly, we have to get to the point where we believe that God is sovereign, and trust that He is. We have to understand and use the tools available to us. "For though we walk in the flesh, we do not war according to the flesh. For the weapons of our warfare are not carnal but mighty in God for pulling down strongholds" (2 Cor. 10:3–4 NKJV). We so often take the probabilities and possibilities and mix them all up to try to figure everything out and assume that it somehow affects reality. How ludicrous we are to assume that we can figure any of it out!

Jonathan stepped out in faith and showed a daring expression of his abandonment into trust that is further indicated by his statement "Perhaps the LORD will help us, for nothing can hinder the LORD. He can win a battle whether he has many warriors or only a few!" (1 Sam. 14:6 NLT).

In Jonathan's mind, the cause was worth his life because he trusted the One who gave him the plan. Simply enough, faith requires action. Quit playing it safe and hiding out under the pomegranate tree because you aren't sure if you will succeed or not. Quit looking to see who's standing with you. If He's called you, then *act*! Abandon yourself to the truth that Jeremiah 29:11 speaks of: "For I know the thoughts that I think toward you, saith the LORD, thoughts of peace, and not of evil, to give you an expected end" (KJV).

Essentially, just trying to survive day to day in life constitutes battle enough. Dodging the bullets of loneliness and "battle fatigue" only compounds the fight. The long and short of it is that you can be like Saul, called to action but betrayed by your own lack of motivation, or you can be a Jonathan, and scale the wall to take on the task directly. Emotionally, physically, and spiritually, you can choose to either hold on to Jesus for dear life with a grip that won't let go, or plummet to your own demise. It doesn't matter your lot in life, sooner or later you are going to have to make a choice of how you're going to take on the fights that will occur. Beware of impulse decisions! It's best to plan ahead on these things. Right answers don't always have invitations or supporters, but the battle isn't yours anyway, so why worry?

"Don't be afraid or discouraged because of this large army. The battle is not your battle. It is God's" (2 Chron. 20:15 NCV).

ᶜ⁓

So true, so true. As singles I think we find ourselves in the thick of the battle more times than we realize.

Back to my fishing trip, which has more to do with battles than you might suspect. We had started our journey on the water at one end of the river and plotted our course to sail to the other end, where a man with a trailer would meet us, take us to our car, and then cart the boat back to its initial location. In the middle of the afternoon, after a delightful time of catching fish and throwing them back, I began to get hungry. Bill paddled us downstream a little farther, where we docked the boat and climbed up a hill to find the most wonderful little restaurant with home cooking. After being on the water and breathing such clear air, all my senses were sharpened. I don't think a meal has smelled or tasted as good since. After completing our meal, we got back in the boat and began to languidly head down the river.

The Big Question

Bill and my friend Jennifer seemed quite at peace with this unhurried meandering, but I began to get slightly uncomfortable. You see, it was beginning to get dark . . . the sun had set in a glorious display, but now that the show was over I was left to ponder my future in this boat. What if something happened to us on the river in the dark? No one would know. I can't swim. Would I drown and be attacked by all those little fish I had harassed with my hook all day? It would be the ultimate revenge . . .

What if? What if? What if? Isn't that the question most singles ask? The battle in our mind is intense. The battle isn't always the type of battle we expect, and that's why we get so thrown off course. The greatest battles most singles fight are the emotional storms within their souls, fraught with concerns about where we're going and if we'll make it. *What if we don't, what will our friends say; even worse, what will our mothers say? Will God keep His promises? Wait a minute. I'm not even clear on what those promises are. What if He didn't mean that none shall lack her mate in the context I put it in? Oh my! Hath God said?* That's the biggie. Ever since Satan asked Eve that question, he has been confronting many a woman. Sometimes it makes you just want to bail, especially when it's getting dark and your days ahead look uncertain. We become overwhelmed with a hunger to know that eventually the desires of our heart will be filled. It is during those times that God sweetly offers us respite to restore our weary souls. He offers a word to nourish us and replenish our capacity to believe once again in the invisible. Then He says, "Get back in the boat; the journey isn't over."

Keeping the Faith

Now there's a time to get out of the boat, and there's a time to stay and hold your peace. I'm reminded of the disciples and their boat stories. First there is Peter, dear brave Peter: "Lord, if that's You out there walking on the water, call me to come to You." It worked for a minute. He was actually walking on water—until he stopped to look at himself. Then he began to sink in the mire of his own shortcomings and inabilities. He was fine as long as he kept his eyes on the Author of his faith. That's exactly when we get in trouble, and the battle begins. We take our eyes off Jesus and begin to look at ourselves. Not just through our own eyes, but through the eyes and opinions of others. We lose our faith footing. We begin to sink in the sea of all the loves that never were and all we presently lack.

Then there is the time when they were all at sea, and Jesus was sleeping in the rear of the boat. A storm arose, and they just lost it. "Master, don't You care if we perish?" Whoo! I'm guilty! "God, don't You see what's going on? Don't You care that I am tired of paying these bills alone? Tired of doing everything for myself? Tired of resisting temptation? Tired of listening to my biological clock? Tired of the succession of battles? Tired of being tired?" That's when I hear Him clearly say, "Well, if you're so tired, why don't you sit down somewhere? The battle is not yours, it's Mine—if you'll allow Me to fight it for you." We, like Peter, get stressed out by our own insufficiencies and fall prey to drowning in the midst of our various struggles, all the while missing the point that we need to get over ourselves and stay focused on the Lord. Sometimes life is much more intense than a fishing trip; however, the principle remains the same, that no matter what type of storm or battle is raging around you, rest and know that Jesus is saying once again, "Peace, be still."

6 Regaining Your Self-Worth

Search me, O God, and know my heart; try me, and know
my anxieties; and see if there is any wicked way in me, and
lead me in the way everlasting.

—PSALM 139:23–24 NKJV

It takes nothing but guts to probe the shadows of our heart and discover what holds us back in life. More often than not, I've discovered that the practice of introspection simply enables me to further chip away at whatever self-worth I have remaining. However, I personally think it's a lonelier process for the single. My assumption is based on the fact that there isn't anyone there to build us back up from the realization of our imperfection. Regrettably, what I have discovered is that lack of self-worth is wrestled with by many of my fellow single friends all over the world, and I imagine there are women in fragile marriages who walk the same lonely path. For this reason, I have laid open my own struggle with you, hoping to reveal some shred of hope for those who regularly wear the facade of perfection while dying on the inside from fear and self-loathing.

To be perfectly honest, this is one chapter I didn't want to write. To lay out struggles and admit faults beyond my grasp was actually more than I anticipated sharing. It's become an offering of transparency and honesty I really didn't intend to make. Furthermore, I feel as if it's convoluted on my part to tutor others on lessons I have yet to learn and vows I myself have never kept. How can I speak with credibility about the very things that can still prove to be barricades in my own life, even today?

Oh, I have read of others who succeeded in the fight, and my heart desires so much to obtain that freedom. However, truth be told, more often than not "the spirit indeed is willing, but the flesh is weak" (Matt. 26:41 KJV). So, while every word of this book mirrors my own passage, this chapter in particular bears the scars and stains of my personal struggle with self-worth. However, I know that I don't walk this road alone and hopefully, by exposing the nasty, gaping wounds occasionally still present in my life, as well as the healed-over scars from victories, I might help others who struggle with this issue in their life. At least, that is my prayer.

LIFE'S PROGRAMMING

With few exemptions, we are brought into this world with equal, healthy, impartial self-images, unprejudiced mental attitudes, and a high level of self-confidence. We all start out with a subconscious mind that is uncontaminated and completely neutral, which will collect and store information from our conscious mind. It will faithfully acquire and dependably dispense back to us any information we put into it, be it constructive or destructive. So essentially, once we take our first gasp of air, our program executes, and the collection process begins, largely dictated by our fallen state.

For the rest of our lives, our luxuriant subconscious mind will serve as a giant sponge, absorbing the world around us. The programming process is completed naturally, with our parents, relatives, teachers, friends, and the media being the primary encoders. These encoders, or programmers, if you will, are things or people who have already developed their own belief systems from sources in their particular lives. Essentially, we are trained to believe what they believe, our mind-set made to reflect their own. Renaissance clergyman and metaphysical poet John Donne captured it best with this insight: "No man is an island, entire of itself; every man is a piece of the continent, a part of the main." I'm not sure this is what he meant, but we are, beyond a shadow of a doubt, bits and pieces of every person we have encountered. Therefore, it makes common sense that our self-image, self-worth, mental attitude, and self-confidence will rise or fall dependent to a large extent on that of our trainers and the things we are exposed to throughout our lives.

So where does this lack of self-confidence, this low self-esteem and the despondent sense of self-worth many singles struggle with come from? Surely, most family members do not purposely program self-loathing and a sense of worthlessness. Teachers are meant to instruct and encourage. How did we develop these negative belief systems or mind-sets about ourselves? Why do most of us live our daily lives with a private self-esteem issue and mediocre (at best) self-image? Is it possible that over time and with the wrong kind of emotional programming, we have come to accept as fact the falsehood that we are not valuable or worthwhile?

THE FIGHT FOR ACCEPTANCE

My actual awareness of self-worth and self-esteem began at a young age when I did everything possible to win attention or affection. I feel as if I have appropriately "earned" the shameful title of "people pleaser." I have seen to it that I accomplished everything in my path, won every award, and met every need of others. However, I have so often lost the "prize" due to circumstances outside my control, which further fed the inferiority complex I had grown to harbor.

I learned the lesson a little too late. It took me years to discover that doing every extra-credit project, skipping recess to clean erasers, and sweeping the floor after school did not win the merit I was so desperately seeking from my peers. The respect I so frantically sought was lost, because I chose works instead of playing dodgeball or their version of *The People's Court* at recess. My attempt to be number one, the best, pushed my peers aside, teaching them rather to dislike me and my aspirations.

Moving into junior high, I didn't have a fighting chance with my peers. Emerging from grade school with the self-reliant "I can take on the world" attitude, despite my inner worries of acceptance and a failing sense of self-worth, I attempted the inconceivable. I ran for student council president. My mom became my campaign manager (self-appointed, mind you), and I basically advertised that I didn't want to win when my mother's campaign slogan hit the streets. It goes without saying that "Vote for Holly, She's So Jolly" wasn't a winning jingle. (Yes, it really happened.) Needless to say, I lost, and I don't remember if I even got any votes, but I'm confident that it couldn't have been too many. I had decorated clothespins for campaign buttons, for crying out loud. I'm not bitter . . . anymore. However, apparently I am still a little traumatized by it.

High school for me brought categorical acceptance, in a wide array. I didn't "fit" into any one grouping of people, rather I was friends with everyone in every grouping. My life in Christ had changed between junior and senior high. I came to a realization at summer camp that I needed to dig down and get serious about my commitment to Him. So, I continued in my trend, adding in my version of Christianity. I played sports, was active in the youth group, and participated in all the extracurricular activities possible. After a serious injury to my right shoulder, I was benched from sports indefinitely.

The problem, I realized years later, was that sports was where I earned so much of my performance-based acceptance. I was good, I knew I was good, and I liked it when everyone else recognized that fact. When I blew out my shoulder, all the acknowledgment disappeared. Needless to say, my self-worth, based on worldly standards and worldly acceptance, was beginning to fade with the accolades I had become so dependent upon. Unfortunately, it was then that my weight started to climb. This was largely due to my nearly constant activity dropping to a few weekly physical therapy sessions because of the constraints of my injury. It was soon thereafter that my programming became destructive and harmful. I was already infuriated with myself because of my injury, and when little jabs regarding my weight started coming from my then boyfriend, well, negativity soon dominated my existence.

INBORN VALUE

With sports out of my reach now, I needed my next acceptance fix. Capitalizing on other gifts, I chose the motivational category on the speech team. With my newfound dedication to Christ, I felt compelled to be a light in the public school circuit. However, my decision to deliver a Christian message in such a circumstance didn't win me much merit. Actually, the message was more for me than anyone else. I meticulously edited chapter four, "The Tale of the Crucified Crook," from Max Lucado's book *No Wonder They Call Him the Savior* into an eight-minute presentation of man's value vs. the world's value. I recommend anything Max writes, but this is a must-read! His premise in this chapter was that somewhere we were sold a bill of goods that man has no destiny or duty, which leads to no value. When Max identified that the world's love is based on appearance and performance, I realized then, *So is my life.* His message that our value is inborn, that we have worth simply because we are, was one I had to grasp personally and then shout from mountaintops.

I smile when I think back to those young days of confidence and assurance. I still have my "rating" sheets from various deliveries of my adaptation of Max's message. I received comments like "A message steeped in religion will not go far in regard to competition" and "I appreciate your attempt to share your impression of the truth; however, I do not believe in God, so your message did not hold water with me." I really didn't care. I had a captive audience of twenty to thirty every time I did my message, and I smiled knowing that I was planting seeds. I believed what I was saying even when I wasn't winning their merit. After all, I had figured out it was better to set my affections on above, and I was actively storing up my treasures in heaven!

College brought more opportunity and a growing sense of value. I was always in the popular crowd. Friendly with everyone, most people on campus knew my name (unfortunately, so did the deans). I was an elected officer of Theta Mu Rho and Sigma Chi Rho (my sororities, if you will) during my four-year stint in school (fortunately, I did much better running for election without a campaign manager) and walked around with undeniable outward confidence. Inside, I started out very steady, but year after year I grew more worthless in my eyes. Oh, I had a personality that would dazzle a prince, but apparently nothing else that would attract a toad. As my friends coupled off and married, my worth, my inborn value I was so sure of only a few years earlier, was regularly up for question.

To be perfectly honest, holding on to Psalm 139:14 (KJV), which affirms that "I am fearfully and wonderfully made," wasn't something I was buying into any longer. Surely there had been a mistake made when it came to me. After graduation came and went, my self-image was in the bottom of the barrel, and my self-worth was valued at about a nickel. I was sure that since I wasn't married, there was something wrong with me. Oh, I had a family that loved me, friends coming out of my ears, and a life that was so amazing and blessed, but discontent with myself grew to be all-encompassing.

A Thorn in the Flesh

After a move to Tennessee, a male friend continually made the comment that two other friends and I made *his* one complete woman, with him selecting the "options" he liked in each of us to complete his ideal companion. Since I wasn't "whole," and no one thought I was good enough to "love," I daily grew to hate myself more and more. When people asked me why I wasn't married or what was wrong with me, I mentally attempted to pinpoint the reason for them. My position of value usually boiled down to my weight, which I had packed on after the sporting accident and the college-imposed "freshman fifteen" a couple of times over. My despair over my size only led to deeper disgust with myself. Ultimately, my self-loathing only drew attention to my character flaws and helped those around me to grow tired of me as well.

Today, it's a slightly different story. I eat healthy, I am active, I work out, I travel and play. I'm still considered "fat" by most people's standards, but I'm in good physical shape, I have fun, and I'm me. More accurately, I recognize those earlier self-demeaning thoughts, that programming, as my "catch," my personal hang-up. I joke about it now as my own "thorn in the flesh," like Paul's in 2 Corinthians 12. First, though, I had to come to terms with the Lord about it. He's brought me to a place where, most days, I don't care if someone around me doesn't accept me. I was prisoner to the old thoughts and reactions for too long. I no longer choose to be ruled by something of such triviality. If I lay around eating bonbons all day, doing nothing, I might be inclined to believe, internalize, and even agree that I was a sloth and worthy of judgment. But that's not my reality.

So when I hear reports that kids in kindergarten, when asked if they would rather be fat or ugly, choose ugly, I smile and shrug it off to bad programming. When the insurance lady denied my request for health insurance coverage because my height and weight were "out of proportion," I laughed it off, taking the blow inside, but capturing the thought I know is meant to disable me and render me useless for Christ. When it's apparent that people do not respect me even though my track record and integrity speak for themselves, I try not to internalize it. Rather, I lay it at the feet of Christ and let it go. While the world judges by the outer appearance, thank God that He judges us by our hearts. After all, I could look fabulous on the outside (by the world's standards that is) and be rotten to the core on the inside. More important, I've realized that my inner beauty transcends my outer beauty. I'm really not too toady or anything, but because of Christ's countenance in me, I'm beautiful even when I'm greasy and grimy on a fishing trip without spackle or anything!

The Full Armor of God

I've learned that in Christ, I am worthwhile, I am valuable, and I do serve a purpose. Capture His essence for yourself. Pull out all the stops . . . say it out loud: "I am worthwhile, I am valuable, I am important—simply because I am." Oh now, we'll forget sometimes; something will try to throw us back to the doldrums of self-pity and worthlessness. But there are tools for us to use minute by minute if necessary.

Gaining control of your thought life will help immensely. However, the first thing to remember is to put on the full armor of God (Eph. 6:13–17). I know it seems a lot like a basic Sunday School class . . . but apparently the basics are what most of us lack! Write His Word upon your heart and use it. My most useful "sword" is Psalm 18:30: "As for God, his way is perfect; the word of the LORD is flawless. He is a shield for all who take refuge in him" (NIV). Whenever I'm facing a serious self-worth issue and I can't just wave it off, I lift my Bible and delight myself in worth and acceptance from my Creator. I bathe myself in choice Scriptures that minister to my spirit and come from the spring of living water. I come out changed, knowing that my life is valuable.

I often reference also my well-worn Beth Moore book *Praying God's Word*. When I fail to remember such things and feel myself slipping into old patterns, I also plug in my favorite movie, *It's a Wonderful Life*. I know it sounds corny and old-fashioned, but I have found that my existence in this world has the George Bailey ripple effect, even when I can't see it. My dog-eared copy of Max Lucado's life-changing book still sits on my nightstand where I can glance at it, refreshed to recall that it's *No Wonder They Call Him the Savior*.

In a scene from the musical hit *The Unsinkable Molly Brown,* Molly says, "I mean much more to me than anybody I ever knew." Healthily place that in the file of self-worth, and trust God for the love you need to be whole. On second thought, I realize that the practice of introspection doesn't really cause me to further chip away at my self-worth; it actually helps me to mine the vein of gold I know runs through the cavern of my soul and allows me to find the prize, the value, I've sought all along.

ℰ∽

Well Holly, we all can go there, can't we? I recall my early years of childhood. It was the most painful time of my existence. You couldn't pay me any amount of money to relive a day. Pathetically thin, buck-toothed—with a wide gap no less—the ugliest glasses my mother could select, and a heavy foreign accent did not make me the most popular girl at school. Well perhaps it did, but not in a good way. So the tape was recorded and replayed early in my mind that I was ugly. Being the survivor that I am, I, too, kicked into performance mode. I was smart, so smart they advanced me two grades ahead, giving the kids in school another reason to hate me. Oh well, too bad for them. It was all I had, and I grabbed the title of overachiever with gusto. If I couldn't have affection, I would settle for admiration. I was doing fine as long as I stuck to my books and was the teacher's pet, but the day came when I made a mistake that scarred me to the present day. Yes, I'm still dealing with it, believe it or not.

DESPERATELY SEEKING APPROVAL

Our Home Economics class decided to have a fashion show with the garments we had made throughout the year. With my mother's help, I had become a rather accomplished seamstress and was quite proud of my lovely, and *different,* creations. I was particularly proud of a little striped number I had concocted. It was a pretty cream-colored skirt (I can still see it in my mind) with soft blue stripes that looked as if they had been hand-painted onto the fabric. I had matched the stripes going down perfectly and then done the pockets and waistband with the stripes going horizontally, while the stripes on the straps were vertical. I thought it was rather clever on my part . . . until I entered the auditorium. There was silence for the longest minute I've ever endured, and then a thunderous roar of laughter. Kids can be so cruel. To this day, I don't know what they found funny. I thought what I had designed was unique, though I was always a bit ahead of my time in terms of fashion. Well, I was mortified and fled in tears, refusing to return for the second show or the encore. The scar was so deep I vowed I would never open myself up for public humiliation again.

God in His graciousness had anticipated this problem. He had already entrenched me deep within the junior high choir production, which came up shortly after the fashion show fiasco, by giving me the main solo because I was the only one who could hit a high C. I would get a low grade if I backed out. It was an obligation I had to fulfill. After throwing up and burying myself in the middle of the choir, I felt that I could make it through the production but vowed never to do it again. The music started, all was going well, and the moment came when I was supposed to hold the infamous note while the rest of the choir vamped around me. I opened my mouth, the note sailed out, and the buzz began. "Who is that? Who is that voice? Look! It's Michelle! Wow! We didn't know she could sing!" *I can sing*, I thought, because they said so. Thus began the pattern of performing for affirmation from others. This is a truly dangerous and slippery place. To rely on what others think of you to define yourself means you will be subject to your confidence rising and falling constantly instead of resting in the knowledge of your own abilities and God's blessing on your gifts. You will be in bondage to others.

The Problem with Opinions

The problem with depending on others' liking what you do is that one day they might not, and you never know when that will be. Here I am, an author/speaker type who still struggles with standing before audiences, but only on the days when I forget why I'm really there—to proclaim the name and the Word of the Lord. It's not about me; it's all about Him. Glorifying the Lord, not glorifying Michelle. Whew! That's a hard one to swallow, isn't it? So God allows our rejection to reveal what really counts. How many people whom we've sought approval from, besides our parents, are still in our lives? It is a futile pursuit, this thing called personal glory . . . oops, I mean acceptance!

You really can't beat yourself up about this too much; 'tis human to crave admiration and acceptance. After all, we are made in the image of God, and even He seeks worship and praise. However, it must be a balanced desire. Our hearts must be set to seek God's favor first. Jesus walked in favor with God and man. Notice the order. However, there came a time when not everyone liked Jesus because of the stand He took, yet He didn't flinch. The only thing that seemed to upset Jesus was the prospect of being separated from the pleasure of fellowship with God. He could stand the heat of unpopularity; it was losing his intimate space with God that was unbearable.

What is most important to you in your search for affirmation and validation? Pleasing the heart of God or man? Jeremiah 17:5 says, "Cursed is the one who trusts in man, who depends on flesh for his strength and whose heart turns away from the Lord" (NIV). If man is distracting you from seeking the Lord's approval, you're in trouble. If man is the focus, you will suffer. People are just too fickle and ever-changing. You can be the flavor of the month for a season and everyone's poison the next.

That person who is celebrating you today might berate you tomorrow. But God is constant and unchanging. He loves you today, and He will love you tomorrow and forever. On that you can depend. In His eyes, you are altogether lovely, because He has washed you with the blood of His Son, Jesus, and covered you with His loveliness, which can never fade. And that, my friend, is a beauty secret the world has yet to manufacture.

7   Everyone Is in Love but Me

For your Maker is your husband, the LORD *of hosts is His name; and your Redeemer is the Holy One of Israel; He is called the God of the whole earth.*

—ISAIAH 54:5 NKJV

Once we enter "grown-up" life (essentially, life past high school), it seems all our single friends begin to disappear, one by one. While I am uncertain as to whether or not I am in an actual race to find my significant other, I am confident (at least most of the time) that singleness is not a disease. Well, at least it is not a contagious disease, I think. However, I do regularly receive e-mails from people asking if I've found a man yet, as if asking me in person could infect them. Other reminders announce new engagements and photos of friends' ever-expanding families, and I pause to wonder what is keeping me from being the sender as opposed to the receiver of such messages. Is there an e-mail with that answer? Can't someone create a meaningful chain letter or "forward" broaching that topic? These occurrences are just a few among many reminding me that I'm getting older, and times are changing. "Everyone" has someone, but I am still alone. Sounds a little like Elijah in I Kings 19:10 and 14, doesn't it?

We turn around and it seems every person we look at is on the arm of a true love, making plans for their future together. Us? We're stuck wondering if we'll ever find that kind of passion. We are spinning our wheels with envy, anger, and a dash of hurt. Fact is, when you are not in love it truly appears as if the whole world is, and you're the only one left standing out in the cold. We walk around trying to conceal our scarlet letter (S for single, not superman) under our oversized coat or sweater, but the searing of the badge goes deeper, to our soul where it just can't be hidden. We try to appear as if we have it all together on the outside. But it doesn't squelch our minds from wandering into the "what-if" sector.

We make pronounced efforts not to exclude ourselves from the goings-on of life. We spend our time laughing (on the outside) when we're with some of those "in love" or newlywed friends, in a dim effort to support them while not ostracizing ourselves. All the while, we are despising our God-given role of the embarrassing third wheel. In spite of this, we muddle through fine until they pause for a romantic interlude. It's then our stomachs really turn. And in a halfhearted effort not to appear jealous, we toss out our best "Oooh, gross!" while inside we long to find our own individual to smooch with on the sidewalk. It constantly lingers in the back of our mind. With all these people "in love" around, it only seems to add anxiety to our already strained "pressure cooker" of a life. And despite the difficulties we endure, singleness really is not a horrible state to be in; however, I will give you that some days it's certainly more difficult than others.

But you know what? Even though we don't have a hot date on Friday or Saturday night, no one to bring us roses or chocolate, we can still have a great love affair going on twenty-four hours a day, seven days a week. Michelle has graciously pointed out over the years that there *is* Someone in my life. Someone who has proved that He would lay down His life for me. He's just and kind, generous and loyal. He said that He'd never leave me, and, well, He's off right now building me a fantastic house! He's coming back for me any day now.

The Big Picture

Hopefully, you have at some point already been exposed to the fact that marriage is a picture of God's relationship with the Christian. Everything from the ceremony to the devotion between husband and wife is displaying the heart and intentions of Christ. All of life here is supposed to be preparing us for our own union with our Maker, at the marriage supper of the Lamb. Our lack of understanding doesn't change the fact that one day He is returning for His bride, the church. The fact that we are preparing ourselves to be Christ's bride is, at times, a hard concept to take hold of. But, keep in mind, we singles who do not have marital experience to draw on (or a poor example through a failed marriage) make efforts to comprehend the depth of God's love for us, but in reality we most likely have a pretty weak understanding of it without the blessing of a mate. It's also pretty tough for us to walk around bragging about our loaded Jewish Fiancé without the four-carat rock that's supposed to support that story.

However, in essence, that is exactly what is to come (not the rock; the marriage, as recorded in Revelation 19. But the rock *is* the foundation!). When I am able to grasp the reality that I am essentially *engaged* to the King of kings and Lord of lords, I'm not sure if I'm thrilled beyond belief or terrified by my own unworthiness. Though I am satisfied and am no longer embarrassed by society's deeming me unworthy, my heart is burdened by my own lack of devotion. I have the perfect soul mate, the Lover of my soul, and quite honestly I often knowingly mistreat Him and do not love Him back well. In fact, I was recently studying the book of Hosea when I noticed an uncanny resemblance between my life and the lives of the Israelites. Despite their deliverance from slavery in Egypt, they chose to embrace idols and other gods to try to find happiness. As I studied the Word, I saw myself in their actions. It's nothing I've consciously done, but I'm guilty all the same. Continually, God has shown me His love, protection, and mercy; and I, as the Israelites were, have been too distracted, too narrow-minded, too stubborn to see His provision and embrace His care and love. I was too focused on my seemingly loveless existence to see Him for who He is . . . the Love of my life.

Why is it so difficult to pinpoint why I so frequently act like the Israelites? Probably because I would prefer that I didn't act like them and would certainly prefer not to recognize all my shortcomings. I would rather pretend it isn't so; after all, no one enjoys being wrong—certainly not the uncaring, unkind person in the relationship. There is a positive here, though, which is that I at least share the Israelites' desire to run back to the Lord (Hos. 14:3). Love's greatest meaning is epitomized here. Even though I am often wrong, as the Israelites were wrong (we both choose our own demigods; today it's things like clothes, friends, work, shopping—whatever we've built up to worship in our lives), the Lord says that He will "forgive them [us] for leaving me and will love them freely, because I am not angry with them anymore" (Hos. 14:4 NCV). I come to my senses and run into His open arms. Where would we be without His grace? David knew the importance of grace, too.

I personally have never been "engaged" to someone, but I've lost a good many friends to the process. Engaged friends start to spend less and less time with their pals and more time with their future mate, because they want to develop and deepen their relationship with their betrothed. They want to get to know this person to whom they have chosen to dedicate their lives. When someone gets engaged, their entire focus becomes the wedding day and life beyond it.

I have literally "stood up" for many different friends, covering about fourteen weddings. (This is no exaggeration; you know the old phrase "Always the bridesmaid, never the bride"?) Well, naturally, I speak from (way too much) experience regarding the preparations and attention that go into the day. (FYI, I've officially retired from being in them now; I just have one on the agenda . . . mine.) Since we will be spending eternity with Christ, does it not make perfect sense for us to take this time to prepare ourselves now . . . spending time with Him and essentially preparing for our future together?

GET A LIFE!

What are you doing with your life? This moment in time, when most of us as singles are free from the overwhelming responsibility of caring for a mate and children, is the perfect time to establish an unparalleled, undivided, unequivocal relationship with Jesus Christ. I view this opportunity in my life as my engagement period. This is the time to learn about and serve the One you love because He first loved you.

However, our betrothal to the most perfect Lover of our soul does not replace our desire for a godly mate while we occupy this world. Do I want a spouse on this earth? Unequivocally, yes. Do I desire to know the love of an imperfect man? Absolutely. Will I settle for second-best? Will I be devastated if I don't ever find him? Not a chance. We are inspired to find someone we can love who loves us back. Someone who will help us better understand the depth of God's affection and how we might bet-ter worship Him, and how to love each other fully. It is accept-able to still have the desire, but the fears and the pangs of loneliness should subside drastically! First John 4:18–19 says, "There is no fear in love; but perfect love casts out fear, because fear involves torment. But he who fears has not been made per-fect in love. We love Him because He first loved us" (NKJV). Be cautious of where you put your love; don't settle for mediocre because you're in love with the *idea* of being in love.

I don't know about you, but I am truly in love with Jesus. He's always a perfect gentleman, waiting for me, not forcing Himself in when He's not wanted. He waits patiently for me, calling and knocking, seeking after me, careful not to intrude but always avail-able—loving me. No, I wouldn't trade Him for anything. I choose to develop a relationship with my spiritual Husband. We can still be waiting for our physical mate, but in that wait we must refuse to allow the "status quo" to dictate our happiness. Revelation 21:2 states the culmination of our lives this way: "Then I, John, saw the holy city, New Jerusalem [our new address], coming down out of heaven from God, prepared as a bride adorned for her husband" (NKJV). Quite simply put, this is a glimpse at the end of the book, the beginning of eternity. Jesus, the untapped Lover of our souls, can often be overlooked by the "unloved" single due to our myopic, self-absorbed focus, but He is there all the same.

HEART CHOICES

So, with everyone being in love limbo around us, we have some choices to make. We can choose to love our Creator, and to love Him well. We can choose to dedicate our life to Him and trust Him with the outcome, hoping it will involve a mate if that is our desire. Or we can choose to hack it through life, pining for a mate in our own strength, ultimately knowing we aren't worthy of one because we can't quite pull our act together even to love God, who loves us unconditionally. By loving poorly, we'll further confound the issue with our own unappeasable expectations and requirements derived from the world. We wouldn't have a fighting chance for a successful marriage based on that. So, the sensible choice is to grow in Christ, allowing Him to cover our life with His timing and His desires, creating a beautiful, valuable treasure to present to our mate.

However, don't be discouraged, because the process of shaping you into this valuable treasure will take your whole life to complete, whether you marry or not. He doesn't want to withhold His plans for you. The good news is that it's not conditional upon who you are today, because Christ stands in the gap as our Advocate, and the Lord has plenty of blessings along the way. Essentially, you will discover that at the end of yourself, you'll find the beginning of Him. It is just plain smart thinking to pursue the perfect Love as the ideal example and preparation for a mate here.

I'm holding to the belief that if I desire successful relationships with others, or a companion who loves me wholeheartedly, the first thing I need to do is love Jesus with all I have. When you look for a mate, find someone who loves Jesus the same way you do. Only His love is flawless; ours is perfected through Him. "If we love one another, God abides in us, and His love has been perfected in us" (1 John 4:12 NKJV). Yes, it appears everyone is in love. Myself included!

℮ↄ

You know what grieves me? (And if it grieves me, it must grieve the true Lover of our souls.) Here we are, created for God's pleasure to worship and adore Him, and we're running all over the place trying to find someone else to love! Ouch! Think about how that must make Him feel. Small wonder that when He found someone who was sold out to Him, He was quick to shower them with blessings. People who spent time with Him, communing with Him and worshiping Him, received riches and favor: Abraham, Isaac, Jacob, David, Solomon, to name a few . . . Not that God is into paying off His friends, but when you truly like someone you want to give them things that will increase their joy if it is within your ability to do so. I love giving my friends presents, because it is an expression of my love for them. I'm sure God feels no differently.

TRUE LONELINESS

Perhaps we don't get the divine connection, so we go in pursuit of our own little treats to fill the empty caverns of our heart, which, unbeknownst to us, are God-shaped, not people- or thing-shaped. We come up empty and ponder why we can't seem to fill the void. Someone asked me the other day, "How do you deal with the loneliness?" I felt bad for her. I knew where she was in her single walk; I've been there, but thankfully I've moved on. I am alone, as in not having a mate, but lonely? Absolutely not.

Let me tell you what true loneliness is: the absence of God. Now, *that* is true loneliness. Adam walked and talked with God every day in the garden by himself and never had a thought about being lonely. Think about it. Adam did not know he was missing anything until God brought it up. There had never been a woman; how would he have known he wanted one? It was God who looked at Adam one day and decided he needed someone. Even after naming the animals and noticing that they all had mates, Adam never asked, "Why does everybody but me have someone?" He merely knew that none of them were like him; there was nothing among them that he desired. No, his fulfillment came from his intimate fellowship with a divine Companion. He was *God*-conscious, not *self*-conscious. Because of this he had the capacity to recognize and love his mate when he was presented with one.

A DIVINE CONNECTION

Let's clear this up now. Your capacity to love the mate God gives you will only match how you are able to love Him. If you are not transparent with God, you will not be able to be transparent with your mate. Practice intimacy with the One who can never lie, who will never leave you or forsake you. The One you will never have to fear rejection from. Practice knowing Him and loving Him.

Ah, but perhaps therein lies the problem. Lost in self-absorption, many people in the world, as well as the church, are not trying to get to know or understand God these days. Most read the Bible as a self-help manual, combing it for principles on how to get what they want from life. It's time to revisit the Word and search for *Him*. To find out every juicy morsel about this Man of ours who plans to return for our hand. What do you really know about Him? If you were getting engaged to a natural man, you would want to know about him before you married him. What does he like to do, what's his family like, what are his dreams and ambitions, how does he feel about you? What's his personality like? Is he kind? Romantic? Faithful? Successful at what he does? You would have a list of things to check to see if the two of you were truly compatible. You would fall in love with him based on his attributes. If you didn't know that much about him, you would not be able to give him your heart, but it's what you know about him and how you feel when you are in his presence that promote loving feelings toward him.

The same is true with God. You cannot love Him if you don't know Him. Time must be spent in the Word of God to learn about Him. Time must be spent in prayer and worship. Have deep conversations in which you speak with Him, and He ministers to your soul. Learn of His heart as you pour yourself out before Him. What is He like? What makes Him laugh, cry, get mad, feel sad? What does God like to do, what is His personality, how does He feel about you? Have you taken the time to learn that He is romantic, sensitive, and responsive? You would know that only if you spent time with Him. Then you would truly fall in love with Him based on what you knew and how you felt in His presence.

Those of us who know Him will not be going to an employee banquet when we leave this earth. We will be attending a wedding feast. *Our* wedding feast. There is no way you can enjoy the honeymoon or even attend the wedding if you are not in love with the Groom. Consider your heart condition. How do you feel about God? Perhaps the loneliness you feel is really your spirit longing to make a divine connection with its Creator. To draw closer to the source of life and love where true wholeness abides, and where you have a love life, too.

God Isn't a Shopping-Mall Santa Claus

My God shall supply all your need according to His riches in glory by Christ Jesus.

—PHIL. 4:19 NKJV

Many would cry foul if they knew how often some of us prayed to the King of kings and Lord of lords for an up-close parking space when it rains. How often do you ask a very important person for a very insignificant thing? (Admittedly, I pray for parking spaces, but I haven't decided if that's wrong or not, since He keeps providing them!) God is concerned with the little stuff, but when we put our requests/demands in perspective, many of our desires are classed with the likes of asking the CEO of a multibillion-dollar company if it's okay to order a sixty-nine-cent ballpoint pen from the supply catalog.

How often do we mumble our newfound "Prayer of Jabez" from rote memory, hoping our magic genie will jump out, instantly granting our wishes and expectations? All of us at times take our long list to God and request away. I think we confuse the verse in which God states that He will provide all our needs to mean He will supply all our greeds! We pray for the perfect mate (with the 199 characteristics we desire); we implore to the Lord that the attractive individual would notice us from across the room. We even call upon Him to save us from having to spend one more miserable Valentine's Day wearing black or one more New Year's Eve without a meaningful kiss at the stroke of midnight. Nearly all of us spend most of our time requesting things of God instead of truly fellowshipping with Him. Rarely do we consistently tap into the deep and meaningful relationship with Jesus we are intended to have. Is that because we really are not sure we know how, or we are too busy hunting for our next request?

How many times have you treated God like a shopping-mall Santa Claus? Do you crawl up into His lap, flash Him a toothy grin, and start going down your wish list? There was a time when, armed with 1 Thessalonians 5:17's "Pray without ceasing" (NKJV) and my long list, I really thought I was in active fellowship with God. I rambled and muttered and invented things to pray for. Needless to say, the people from Asia all the way to Zambia were covered! Somewhere along the path of my spiritual existence, I missed the point of fellowship. I was so busy praying for everything under the sun that He could not get a word in edgewise! I really didn't understand the concept of fellowshipping with God. Psalm 46:10 (NKJV), "Be still, and know that I am God," just caused confusion.

MARTHA, MARTHA, MARTHA

Since I was about fifteen, I have been active in some form or fashion of ministry. Whether teaching a vacation Bible school class, an Awana or neighborhood Bible club, a Bible study group, or traveling around the country with Christian artists, I have been serving Christ. The only problem with my active servitude is that there have been occasions when I was so busy *serving* Christ, I completely sacrificed my time of *being with* Christ. When push comes to shove, I am more Martha, scurrying about making sure everything is right, even though I know I need to be more like Mary, sitting at His feet, learning.

I have also shared that I personally have trouble with the little two-letter word *no*. Ironically, it was my first word, but somewhere along the line I forgot how to use it. I am a worker bee who says yes to everyone because I undeniably struggle with the need to please people. This all translates to a schedule that has been out of control in the past. It was not uncommon for me to work straight through from 8:00 A.M. until 2:00 the next morning. I would eat meals at my desk and not move if I was "in the zone." I worked nonstop!

I have been in church pretty much my whole life. I grew up with the luxury of those illustrious flannel graphs and great teachers. I knew the Ten Commandments and cannot really offer any reason why I chose to disregard number four: "Remember the Sabbath day, to keep it holy. Six days you shall labor and do all your work, but the seventh day is the Sabbath of the LORD your God. In it you shall do no work" (Ex. 20:8–10 NKJV). I ran around working for Jesus, and I ran and I ran some more. Not *from* anything or *to* anything really, just in my little circle world of work and ministry and ministry and work.

While I looked for downtime, my "less hectic schedule" always remained on the horizon. I kept pushing forward. After running in circles for a couple of years and unselfishly disclaiming the Sabbath commandment with the fact that I was, after all, doing it for His glory, all the days of rest that I missed caught up with me at once. The Lord knows His children require rest.

Psalm 23:2–3 says, "He makes me lie down in green pastures, he leads me beside quiet waters, he restores my soul" (NIV). I firmly believe that God sometimes has to change our circumstances just to get our attention—to make us understand. Rest is something that is built into our lives on purpose (Gen. 2:2–3). In fact, every poor decision I've made in my life has been when I have been exhausted and not thinking clearly.

A Lesson Carved in Stone

My lesson couldn't have come at a poorer time, which is why I think He chose it. I was watching my friends' son while they skied out west when I came down with a searing pain in my side. I have a very high threshold of pain and have sports injuries stories that would make most faint. I'm my father's daughter who never goes to the doctor and is rarely sick. But when the pain started, I tried my dad's theory of walking it off, to no avail. I completed my work at my day job . . . through the pain. I then had a meeting downtown for my second "ministry" job, of which I could not tell you one thing discussed. I just remember the pain smarting so much, I spent most of the meeting time in the rest room, hunched up in a corner.

After the meeting concluded, I picked up the baby from another friend's home and was back on "Aunt Holly" duty. Fortunately, Cooper always has been a dreamboat child and was content to watch Veggie Tales while his aunt Holly writhed in the bed trying to find a comfortable position. Unfortunately, I never found one. Needless to say, the night culminated in a visit to the emergency room where I was admitted within minutes. I spent the next seven days of my life in the hospital there. Of course, Murphy's Law prevailed, and a quick in and out was not in the plan. My schedule did not accommodate plans for *any* hospital stay, let alone a seven-day stint. Please understand, I was due to close on my newly constructed home in exactly one week, I had clients to juggle, work to be done, and forms to be signed. No, not at all a good time for this.

Long story short, I had a boulder of a kidney stone that was too large to pass without an invasive procedure. Since this was my "lesson" (which cost considerably more than my college tuition, now that I think about it), of course I had complications from the surgery. My parents rushed to be by my side, my friends visited me in the hospital, and I had flowers and cards in abundance. I was loved, but I was alone and miserable at night. It was in the quietness of those nights, however, that the Lord opened up sessions in the school of hard knocks.

He was tender, and I knew I'd had several warnings that probably would have spared me from this debacle, but I was stubborn, and essentially too busy to listen, until then. It was in those quiet evenings alone that I learned what it meant to be still and know that He is God (Ps. 46:10). I finally learned to be the sheep and listen to my Shepherd's instruction. I was at long last able to recognize His voice, and actually allowed Him to do the speaking for a change. Ultimately, I was catching up on my Sabbaths for the past few years in one extended "break." I firmly believe it was basically so I could be trained in what it means to rest in Psalm 16:5: "LORD, you have assigned me my portion and my cup; you have made my lot secure" (NIV). I was trying to manage everyone's portion, but I was responsible for only mine!

DWELLING IN THE SECRET PLACE

Nowadays, I still work too much sometimes, but I have learned the dirty word *no* and even use it sometimes. I consciously try to set aside one day out of the week to rest, even if my "to do" list is twenty pages long. I've resigned myself to the fact I'll never get it all done. I've also learned that we truly need to make the Lord our priority and rest in Him, even when we are too busy. Granted, I had to make a concerted effort to make that happen, and you might just need to do that, too.

I have a hammock between two trees in my backyard where I often go just to sit and fellowship with my Creator. I no longer ramble off prayers pages long; sometimes I just sit and think about Him and heaven, which refreshes me beyond belief. Sometimes I worship Him by singing praise songs over and over again, speaking my love and exalting His name while I rock in the wind, in the middle of His creation.

No matter what I do when I'm out there, in the end I just sit back and bask in His presence. I stop and listen for His still, small voice. It's a lot easier to hear now that I've learned to hold my tongue a bit. Truth be told, I have had more revelations in my backyard since I got that hammock than in any of the numerous years before that. It is the place where I go to fellowship, to retreat from my crazy life full of e-mails, day timers, cell phones, and pagers.

I encourage you to create a place like that for yourself. A prayer closet of sorts. Choose to dwell in the secret place of the Most High, abiding in the shadow of the Almighty (Ps. 91:1). He has created this haven specifically to protect us while we fellowship and are refreshed in His presence. He wants to fill us with His strength and vigor so we can face the world as a strong witness for Him. Granted, I still have my prayer lists of things that need to be lifted up—for friends, decisions, and other things— and I still have my own twisted views on what I want or need, but I have misused my privilege of approaching the throne in greed for the last time (unless parking spaces count).

Transformation

Lately, I start my requests with the appeal that His wish list fully replace my own; that my mind would be transformed to His mind. I've finally quit self-prescribing the solution to my problems. He's wanted to robe me in His finest silks and linens and teach me that His ways are higher than my ways for so long, and I've finally come to the place where I actually let Him garnish me with the honor of being His child. These days, He knows I'm there to lay down some burdens and do some groaning, sure, but He knows that in my heart I'm really there just to love Him. Today, I run out to my hammock. I climb up into my Dad's lap with my list and yeah, I still flash Him a toothy grin. But now, it's not so I can melt His heart to get my way, it's just so I can melt His heart with my love (see Song 4:9).

❧

Hmm . . . I often think to myself, *Poor God. Most folks don't want to talk to Him until they need to. Or until they want something.* The idea is that God is there for their benefit, with no thought of blessing God at all. It's the Santa Claus syndrome. Then there's the crowd who talk to Him because they know they should, so they repeat the same thing over and over again. I'm sure they bore Him to tears if that is possible, and then finish with a flourish as if they've done God a favor by speaking to Him. They miss out on such joy: the pleasure of having God's Spirit communicate directly with theirs, to share secrets, hidden things that are not apparent to the eye. When I read things in the Bible such as God's telling Moses He would fulfill his request because Moses was His friend, it just blows my mind! Can you imagine God saying, "Hey Michelle, I'm going to do that for you because you are My friend." That gives me chill bumps.

Up Close and Personal

Just remember this: Even with Santa Claus, you've got to crawl up into his lap to tell him what you want. I remember when I was a little girl crawling up into Santa's lap and becoming thoroughly enraptured with how cushy and comfortable he felt. The whiteness of his beard. The deepness of his voice, the twinkle in his eyes. And how good his arms felt wrapped around me. And that laugh! How I loved that laugh! It almost made me forget what I wanted. But finally, I'd deliver my list. I never stopped to think that Santa might want something, too. It was his job to give me the desires of my heart . . . kind of like God, huh? On one level Santa Claus is kinda like God when you think about it. Santa had to be pleased with us in order to give us what we wanted. After all, he had to find out if we were naughty or nice. He wouldn't deliver his presents while we were looking! Noooo! We had to rest, go to sleep, to give him the opportunity to deliver our gifts—that was the hardest part! All we could do was pray that Santa liked us and would give us what we'd asked for.

I think most of the time we prefer to stick to our lists and dash out of the throne room, avoiding God's presence, never mind His lap, because we're afraid of what God might say to us. You see, intimacy will always be followed by revelation when we get up close and personal with God. And you better bet your bottom bippy that revelation is going to demand some change on our part. It might actually make us change some of the things on our long lists of requests. And let's face it, we don't want to change. We want to stay the same and have God be like Santa Claus and cooperate with our program. Just give us what we want. Bless our mess. We want Him to just do what we tell Him, even though we refuse to admit it. The only person that misses out in this equation is us, if we're guilty.

I recall the Lord telling me one day that I would be better off single than married. "How could You say such a thing, Lord?" I exclaimed. "Because when I tell you to do something," He said, "you can pretend that you didn't hear Me and continue doing as you please. But if you had a physical husband standing in your face, you would struggle with submission, because you have not perfected it with Me." Oooh! I was mortified! Cut to the quick! All I could do was hang my head and vow to do better. He tested me on it weeks later by asking me to deny myself something I had been coveting for a long time. I am happy to say I passed the test of obedience and have continued to improve when it comes to paying attention to His still, small voice. However, this is probably the greatest dilemma of the single life. We love to be busy because we don't want to stay still long enough to deal with our aloneness. We don't want to stop long enough to hear what God has to say because He might tell us we have to stay in this state longer than we would like. So we just wear ourselves out and avoid the entire subject.

We like to keep God at arm's length because we don't want Him to have that much access to our lives. However, when we don't we rob ourselves of rest. We have no idea what is coming up in our lives. When we hit a storm we spend all our energy backpedaling out of it in the flesh. There is a daily rest besides the Sabbath that God wants us to enter into. I was always struck by the fact that no matter what Jesus encountered—demonically possessed people, hostile leaders, fickle crowds, top brass, leading intellectuals, tempting women, or the devil himself—He was always as cool as a cucumber. He was always at rest, at ease, unruffled. Why? Because He had spent time talking to the

Father and was well prepared to meet the dramatic events each day brought.

The Blessing of Preparation

I kind of get a picture of God saying to Jesus one morning, "Son, today You're going to run into the man who's been infested by a legion of demons. He's going to be quite a sight; things could get out of control if You appear flustered. You know how demons are; they get boisterous if they think they've pushed Your buttons, so just stay calm, order them to go into the pigs that will be grazing nearby, and everything will be cool." So when the whole thing went down Jesus was unfazed by the ordeal because He was already suited up and prepared to handle it!

God wants to give us the weather forecast for our lives every day so that we, too, can be in a constant state of rest. This, however, does not cancel out the importance of taking the time to nurture at least one day of rest a week as well. If God needed to take a day off, what is your malfunction? Are you greater than He who created everything, including you and me? I don't think so.

I used to ponder His promise to cause us to walk on the high places of the earth if we would keep the Sabbath holy and turn away from doing for our own pleasure on that day. I asked, "Why, Jesus, is that so important to you?" Let me tell you what He showed me. When you lay aside your own agenda you're open to finally hear what God has in mind. Going to church on Sundays is not just about your going to get something from God—a word to prop you up for the week or a new revelation you were too lazy to glean for yourself. Come on now, sometimes we just don't want to do the work, or simply don't know how. Anyway, going to church is initially about your going to the temple to bring your worship and praise to God. To empty out your heart and soul to Him. It is when we pour out that He comes down to refill us. Fresh living water restores our souls. As we go forth, we should allow that water to sit and refresh our spirits. It just doesn't happen if you dash off to the mall to finish your weekend shopping or whatever activities fill your Sundays. I'm not insisting that Sunday be the day, but you do need one day of doing nothing to simply hear the voice of the Lord, to allow Him to minister to your inner man or woman. Even if you spend the whole day at home in your jammies, you will be surprised at the difference it will make.

THE BENEFITS OF REST

First of all, you will feel better. Ready to tackle the rest of the things on your plate, which, by the way, haven't gone anywhere while you took your day off. Refreshed, you will be able to do a good job at whatever you have to do; therefore, you will prosper. You will walk on the high places of the earth. Promotion follows excellence; excellence comes from a sharp, grounded spirit. Your attitude will be better after a good rest as well. Tempers won't rise at the slightest irritation. I know you can hear me on this. We all can relate to being in overdrive for indefinite periods of time where we fear blowing our gaskets. We say to ourselves, "When will this ever end?" I'll tell you. When you call a halt to it, and not a moment before.

Feeling overworked, underpaid, and loveless on top of it all? Perhaps it's time to stop, look, listen to your heart and hear what it's saying. Your heart would be honest and tell you what's really lacking: entering into the rest of the Lord. He, like Santa Claus, is sure to deliver incredible gifts, if we give Him the time and the space to do so.

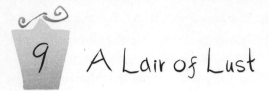

9 A Lair of Lust

I betrothed you to one husband, that to Christ I might present you as a pure virgin.

—2 CORINTHIANS 11:2 NASB

I really don't like to talk about s-s-sex. I would actually like to pretend that it doesn't exist since it doesn't technically apply to me right now. First Corinthians 6:12–20 has me shaking in my boots. I'm a rule follower on stuff like that. Sex is so intimate and so private that it feels wrong to even mention it. Then I nod my head as I remember that the television and movie theaters display the act graphically nearly hourly with seemingly little or no thought for our moral state. Even when I avoid the picture tube and movies, there are always the kids at the mall who are openly doing things my mother would turn me over her knee for thinking, let alone acting upon. And then there is where I spend half my life, the airport. I am regularly assaulted with reunited lovers attempting tonsillectomies on each other right there in the baggage claim area. Gasping for air (me and them both), my eyes roll and my stomach turns. However, truthfully, my mind is awakened to full-lust "wonder and wish" mode while witnessing the above violations to my personal regard. Serious eye rolling!

In light of all that, I know I should be less embarrassed and really ought to become more comfortable with the idea of discussing sex (like a grown-up) from a biblical perspective. It's apparent to me that those supporting the "free love" movement have had no qualms about flaunting it, so I should be as open about preserving it. In my limited understanding of the whole process, it boils down to this: God made sex for beauty, intimacy, and worship, but society as a whole has cheapened it to lust, perversion, and ugliness. Now, given a choice, what camp would get your registration?

Have you ever stopped to wonder why we are so fascinated with fairy tales like *Sleeping Beauty, Snow White,* and *Cinderella?* Walt Disney established an entire media kingdom based on the world's acceptance of fantasy. Even now, those images frequently run pleasantly through my mind. Only I am the princess waiting to be rescued, and my prince is just off in the horizon and will arrive in the nick of time to sweep me off my feet, someday. Often, the fairy-tale ending is all that keeps us going, the innate promise that some day we will live happily ever after.

So why have we bought into that as an ideal? It's simple, really. Everyone wants the happy ending. Unfortunately, as life (and deception) plays out, circumstances, emotions, and loneliness dictate how our world evolves, and it's rarely what we've envisioned it to be. It's sad to us when it doesn't resemble the fairy tale we have scripted for ourselves. So we come to the place where we make concessions and trades to attempt to make our own happiness, regularly with detrimental results despite our best efforts.

Buying the Lie

Regrettably, most often we buy the lies and walk headlong into the trap of some kind of sexual relationship where we often cheapen our own value and worth through our actions. We betray our future hopes, desires, and dreams for the pleasure of the moment. Media moguls have successfully convinced us there is nothing wrong with and no penalty for any form of casual sexcapade. Of course, they are presenting only half the facts. But why would they change an award-winning campaign that is "selling" to millions around the world?

Unfortunately, I've found among my peers, and the generations that have followed, it is very common to completely miss the mark and settle for the half-truths that surround us. It's easy to do since we are completely inundated with such misleading notions in every way. However, I firmly believe that by consenting to sexual relations outside marriage, we not only hurt the Lord, but also our future mates and ourselves. "So run away from sexual sin. Every other sin people do is outside their bodies, but those who sin sexually sin against their own bodies" (1 Cor. 6:18 NCV). All throughout the Word, sexual sins appear to be the only ones specifically aimed at our bodies. The detrimental effects, mostly unseen, can take a lifetime to heal. There is an emotional and physical transformation an individual goes through in the giving of oneself. It's something that can't be calculated on any scale or measured in any lab. However, we are called to holiness, and being holy is about being His—not sacrificing ourselves on the table of gratification. Past abuse, consensual promiscuity, or even a single mistake can wreak havoc on our justification system, and once we've stumbled onto the road, we mistakably assume that we are on the path of no return. Soon thereafter, we rationalize that there is nothing left to protect, so why not indulge the lusts of our nature.

I suppose what shocks me most is that, even in Christian circles, premarital intimacy has become common and acceptable. "Common," I can agree to. Yes, it is very "common"; in fact, very ordinary and status quo. However, "acceptable," I'll never support. Sexual sins are tenacious sins against our soul, mind, spirit, and body. You simply cannot justify the act of sexual relations with "Well, everyone else is doing it," because, guess what . . . I'm not, which puts holes in your theory off the bat! Get a grip on reality! Please understand that lust will not transition to love, and love is certainly more than a sexual experience. In fact, let's look at a picture of true love.

Living the Fantasy

Disney has nothing over the story portrayed in the Song of Solomon. In fact, I enjoy the imagery of this book so much that I aspire to have a relationship with someone exactly like what is pictured here, not a cheapened version of it or a backseat romance. Why would we want anything less for our lives?

Think about what is construed to be "love" in our lives. Then look at the beauty here. What woman in her right mind wouldn't want her two breasts to be like two fawns or her thighs to be likened to jewels? (I will pass on the hair like a flock of goats, however!) I want my love to hold the same confidence as that shown in Song of Solomon 7:10: "I am my beloved's, and his desire is toward me" (NKJV).

How can we have such a relationship? One little verse seems to make the difference: "I charge you, O daughters of Jerusalem, by the gazelles or by the does of the field, do not stir up nor awaken love until it pleases" (Song 2:7 NKJV). I can't help but point out that this little line is so important it's repeated in Song of Solomon 3:5 and 8:4.

Fellow singles, do not rouse or waken love until the designated time. Let me clear up the wonder right now. What is the designated time? Simply this: when you meet your prince or princess and you enter into the covenant relationship of marriage. *Period.* That is the only time *any* form of sex should be awakened. That is the designated time. Not when you get engaged, not on a first date, and not once you feel comfortable. It's when you've entered into a marital commitment and not a moment sooner.

This isn't just something I've come up with on my own. The Bible speaks several times on sexual relations being within the confines of the marital relationship. "'For this reason a man shall leave his father and mother and be joined to his wife, and the two shall become one flesh' . . . So then, they are no longer two but one flesh. Therefore what God has joined together, let not man separate" (Matt. 19:5–6 NKJV). Sexually speaking, the two will physically become "one flesh." "One flesh" is used here to denote the consummating sexual act of marriage. God's intended exclusiveness of the one-flesh relationship disallows any other relationship. This eliminates homosexuality, polygamy, adultery, premarital sex, and incest. Essentially, these and other sexual actions violate the "oneness" of the marriage relationship.

In Old Testament times these violations were liable to be punished by death (Lev. 20:1–19; Deut. 13–26; Rom. 1:26–32). Hebrews 13:4 says, "Marriage is honorable in all, and the bed undefiled: but whoremongers and adulterers God will judge" (KJV). Look at 1 Corinthians 7:2: "Nevertheless, to avoid fornication, let every man have his own wife, and let every woman have her own husband" (KJV). The word *fornication* here is from the Greek word *porneiva,* which is translated as "illicit (not permitted or allowed) or unlawful sexual intercourse." Ironically, this is also where we get the word *pornography,* which is another form of sin that is a perverted twist on God's best.

LET SLEEPING DOGS LIE

What's happened is that we've awakened "love" prematurely. We have been strategically led to believe that sex is the one element that must be present to obtain the much sought-after perception of earthly love. However, instead, we have gained an appetite for lust. Our appetites are what drive us. We are designed so that when we become hungry, we eat. In the same way, our sexual appetites are being stimulated through our eyes and ears . . . awakened before their time. Movies, books, magazines, billboards, television, and other media are designed to entice and encourage hunger in this area. Consider Proverbs 4:23–27:

> Above all else, guard your heart, for it affects everything you do. Avoid all perverse talk; stay far from corrupt speech. Look straight ahead, and fix your eyes on what lies before you. Mark out a straight path for your feet; then stick to the path and stay safe. Don't get sidetracked; keep your feet from following evil. (NLT)

Sexual abuse, graphic images, promiscuity, and peer pressure are things that are further aiding the trend of premature sexual relations in our lives and the lives of youth today.

Stop and consider the diet of programs you've watched or magazines you've read in the past few weeks. How do your viewing habits (which indicate how well you are guarding your heart) measure up to the Proverbs passage quoted above? Are you unintentionally sidetracking yourself without even being aware of it? Feasting on soft pornography and explicit language through the stuff we put in front of ourselves will only awaken the lust in us. It's entirely possible that a diet full of this trash has awakened our senses and wonder into physical actions. However, it's becoming more and more imperative that we, as believers, deliberately and consciously set ourselves apart for Him. You need to ask yourself, "Am I ready to take my grade A loins off the meat market? Am I ready to quit sacrificing my mind and/or body for lust and desire, choosing rather to wait on God's plan, which is for a true and pure love?" If so, we need to consciously put aside all contemptible things that daily chip away at our resolve. For myself, I've learned that I have to abstain from sexual temptations, flee those images, and abandon the theology of the world, or my mind becomes inundated with the sludge of such things.

Personally, I've chosen to wait to have sex. I prefer to wait until I can make love and it really be that. Many would say that is pretty unrealistic, but I have sources that confirm it is worth the wait. My ability to remain pure until the day we can join together as one is the beginning of who I am for my mate. Even playing the devil's advocate, allowing that such a thing is common or typical, I know my choice is head and shoulders above mall make-out sessions and backseat romances, which inevitably lead to pain and hurt. Regardless, there are days when I feel all alone in my solemn vow, my necklace of commitment pinching at my neck.

For this thirty-year-old virgin (who hasn't always made all the best choices in every situation) who has been saving herself for her husband, it's not an easy road. I often joke with my inner circle of friends that they need not call me for the first year I'm married. Because, I *will* be busy making up for all this lost time. However, as I said, staying abstinent in our society isn't easy. I personally have made a commitment to be worthy of the white dress I will wear on that day. While I have that allegiance as my foundation, I am finding the commitment becomes more challenging and more difficult to hold on to with each passing year.

SEX BY DESIGN

The first thing to realize is that sexual intimacy isn't the purpose of desiring a husband. Too often we summon the verse "It is better to marry than to burn" and rush ahead of the plan. But the ultimate intention of marriage is so that you as a couple can say, "Oh, magnify the LORD with me, and let us exalt His name together" (Ps. 34:3 NKJV). It's that two would be stronger than one. In light of this, I desire to come to my marriage bed with the pure gift of myself for my husband. This is what helps me stand firm in my commitment even in the most passionate of moments.

Most days we don't want to cope as the apostle Paul did. When our hormones are raging and our heart cries for children, personally, I'd rather trade in my singleness "red badge of courage" for that nuclear family of 4.5 that drives a minivan and lives the proverbial 8.6 miles from the city. It's not wrong to yearn for those things, but where my perspective lies and how I deal with those desires make all the difference. Satan has all the signs in place that point to such dreams, but they seem to be leading only to a path of hurt, abandonment, and destruction. While Satan's sexual advertising campaign is in full-blown heavy rotation, believe me when I tell you that sex is not the way to attract or catch someone worthy of your life. If you cannot attract someone with your heart and mind then your body will not be able to hold them for long. Remember that a whoremonger will attract a whoremonger. A prince is looking for a princess.

Accountability is another essential element of remaining pure. To be able to enjoy dating or courting and remain sexually pure, you must have people in your life to whom you can be accountable. These must be individuals who hold the same belief—that sex is designed for marriage. It's a long and winding road, but the destination is unparalleled. It is wise to place people around you who will ask you the tough questions and hold you to a higher standard of living.

So what about those of you who have already blown it? You were not able to abstain from the pressures and have already encountered a premarital sexual situation. You've walked the road and become sexually active with someone (whether it be oral sex or actual intercourse), and now you are struggling. The first thing to remember is that it does not make you a bad person. While you haven't made the best decisions, God is a very gracious God. First Corinthians 6:18–20 tells us to flee from sexual immorality and encourages us to honor God with our body. For anyone who has had a sexual experience outside marriage, the guilt it conjures up can be overwhelming. However, if your sexual experiences plague you, it's time to accept God's forgiveness and make a commitment to remain abstinent going forward.

Only God can cleanse us and wash us. God cannot resist broken children who really love and worship Him. He can and will take all things old and make them new again. Although you will still live with the natural consequences of your actions, God will forgive you if you seek that from Him (Ps. 103:12). You have to confess and repent of your sins. Ask Him to forgive you for being careless with this gift. Ask Him through His grace to remove the lust, and restore love in your life. Agree with Him that your actions cannot be justified, but ask that they be forgiven.

If you allow Him, in time His grace will do a healing work in you. However, what you have done is awakened desires in your life that are further fed by the mental images and sensory responses your body has encountered. When those feelings of desire come, and they will, you have to train yourself to use them to rouse a desire for God instead of the urges they awaken now. The key is to turn what the enemy wants to use to control and degrade you into something that will actually encourage and enhance your relationship with Christ.

Let your struggle in this area lead you to find some accountability partners who can help you stay on track spiritually and help you avoid yielding to sexual temptation. You will need to seek God and pray for a hunger and thirst for Him to replace these desires. Throughout this book you've seen how desire for anything less than God leads to sin and struggle. God is offering to us the option of transformation. He's inviting us to crave Him more than anything else in this world. If we do, we will find the freedom to walk in His call. He will equip us for the battle.

DECISIONS, DECISIONS

I think the key to avoiding premarital "stuff" is best viewed in action. Genesis 39 begins with Joseph, who was just literally sold out by his merry band of brothers. Subsequently, he has been purchased as a slave for Potiphar's house. Proceeding through the chapter, we find Joseph quickly climbing the corporate ladder within the infrastructure where he lands as the number two guy in the land. But as usual, Satan is around the corner with the trip wire. Genesis 39:7 is where we find Potiphar's wife ogling the new guy Joseph, attempting to play the role of seductress. Day after day she tries, but Joseph's example stands. *Flee!* (Gen 39:12). Second Timothy 2:22 also advises us to "flee from youthful lusts" (NASB). *Flee* is a pretty strong word. In other words, don't stick around for the inevitable. You are in trouble, and the only answer is to run!

If you are sitting there wondering just how far you could go before you'd stand in judgment, quite simply you may need to revisit your commitment to the Lord. If you're still skulking around in the darkness, it's time to turn on the Light. The key is not how close you can skirt the edge, but how you can best honor your body. However, if you are looking for a guideline to communicate to your boyfriend, what personally works for me is that I can go only as far as I would feel comfortable if my father were in the room. See, dads are the spiritual heads of the household as well as the protectors. If you don't have a father figure in your life, or have only a poor example, place your spiritual Daddy in that spot. How far would you be willing to go with Jesus on the couch with you? Most papas wouldn't want you to do anything past holding hands, and that's a very safe and realistic place to leave it. For me, a peck hello or a quick kiss good night is manageable, but honestly, I don't trust myself in make-out sessions, which more often than not lead to an area I choose not to go. That's when I flee!

I think the best way for us to grasp the process of purity in singleness is to allow ourselves to be viewed as treasured pearls. Reminiscent of our lives, "natural" pearls only form in about one out of every forty pearl oysters. Many of us will force ourselves into simulated contentment and mock understanding but will never really come to rest in the truth. Most will slip into the pleasure the world offers and settle for the counterfeit solution. Sadly, there are many forged and cultured pearls out there and, quite candidly, most average people wouldn't be able to tell you the difference from just looking at one, but there is a difference, a very large one.

For any pearl to develop, there first has to be an irritant. For singles, we can easily place our unaccompanied status as the aggravation, even if we don't always perceive or admit that we see it that way. In the beginning stage of the pearl's astonishing creation, the little annoyance is generally an ordinary grain of sand. It is nothing large, just something not quite right, not normal, not accepted. In order for the irritant to be "coped" with, the clam, oyster, or mussel will secrete a coating substance known as nacre.

As such, we can allow God's love to serve as the nacre to coat the annoyance (our singleness) purely, or we can slap on our own coating of relationships, sex, fantasy, and false humility. His coating has uniform color distribution, high luster, and is essentially free from flaws. Our coats, however, lack the translucent quality of the natural process, contain blisters and pits of imperfection, and produce a product that is slightly out of round.

Gemologists will tell you that the more valuable pearls are ones that develop naturally and grow slowly, allowing the nacreous secretion to form a shell lining over and over again. Luster, color, shape, and size are all considerations in the final valuation of the treasure. If a pearl is forced to form too quickly or is plucked too early, that can and most likely will affect the final appraisal. Lives are like that—sacrificed potential at the hands of impatience. While all of us try to coat our own wounds, if we take them to the Lord to heal, we will have a superior, more valuable final product. Oh, we can fake it, we can do it ourselves, but it will always produce a counterfeit, a life of lesser quality. Still of value, still worthwhile, but not all that it could be.

ベ

Well girl, I don't know what to add to that. I couldn't have said it better myself. However, you know I can never stay speechless for long. Let me just insert this. If you are struggling with your hormones, the struggle won't end when you're married if you don't get control now. If you can't keep your body for God, are you really sure you can keep your body for your husband? "But that's different, Michelle," I heard someone say. No, it's not.

BE FAITHFUL

Jesus is your Fiancé. Most women who have a physical fiancé don't sleep around. They are preparing themselves, anticipating their wedding night. We gasp in horror when a guy has a last fling before his wedding and gets an STD or is discovered by his mortified bride. "Oh! That terrible man," we say, yet many don't stop to consider that is what they are doing when they give their bodies to someone who does not have the approval stamp of "husband" from God.

Trust me, God has nothing against sex. After all, it was His idea. And every idea He had was "good." But He *does* have a problem with sex in the wrong context. To God, sex before marriage is considered not only fornication, but also adultery. That's right, ladies, He says that you are cheating on Him! After all, He is your Fiancé. If you can't remain faithful to the perfect mate, how can you remain faithful to an earthly one? What would happen if your mate was injured, or made you angry, or was gone for a long period of time? Would you be able to wait on him? What if Mr. Absolutely Wonderful flirted with you during your time of separation from your mate? Would you be able to remain faithful both mentally and physically? Then why can't you wait on the Lord?

But it's been such a long time, Michelle. You don't understand . . . whine, whine, whine . . . Mmm, its hard for me to feel sorry for you when I've probably been waiting longer than you. The point remains, your body does not belong to you. It belongs to God, therefore you don't get to do with it as you please. Remember, He is watching.

RELEASING THE POWER

Yes, you have been purchased. Bought with a price. Jesus sacrificed His life to redeem yours. "Present your bodies, a living sacrifice . . ." Remember that one? God regards sex as an act of worship. The person you give your body to becomes your lord and master. You become a bond slave. You've submitted yourself to him. The term used for sexual intimacy in the Bible is "know." Genesis 4:1 says that "Adam knew Eve his wife, and she conceived" (NKJV). He knew her in the sexual sense. When you allow someone to know you like that, to know your deepest, most inward being, you are releasing your power into their hands. It's like giving away a secret that could be used against you.

Whoever has your body also has your mind. Sex is powerful; it can reduce the strongest and the most intelligent beings to blubbering idiots. Look at the person who is presently tempting you. Is this someone to whom you want to give that much power? Is he worthy of your worship? Hmm, that puts another spin on it, doesn't it?

Consider Samson, a full-blooded strong man. He was able to route an entire Philistine army all by himself with the jawbone of a donkey, but was reduced to putty by the sexual favors of Delilah. He completely lost it. His fear of God, his discernment, his sight, his freedom, and finally his life. Premarital sex costs too much. I don't know about your budget, but I'd rather spend my money elsewhere on something with more of a guaranteed return. Something lasting. Something my heavenly Father will bless.

What will He bless? A life that is totally devoted to Him. A life of pure worship. If you're searching for the answer to hormones run amuck, this is it. Turn your focus toward worshiping God. Lust is no match for worship. As you begin to pour yourself out to the Lord, He will meet you and satisfy your deepest desires. He will fill you with Himself, with His peace, joy, and fulfillment. And trust me, His touch is far more lasting.

10 Finding Your Purpose

Two people are better than one, because they get more done
by working together. If one falls down, the other can help
him up. But it is bad for the person who is alone and falls,
because no one is there to help.

—ECCLESIASTES 4:9–10 NCV

The overwhelming pressure from family, friends, and general well-wishers to produce a mate to validate our status in life is driving us crazy! Inaccurate quotes on our chance of marriage after a specified age only add to the distraught nature of our apparent failure. The mountain one travels over to reach contentment is conquered one step at a time. Currently, we spend too much time basking in our own self-pity, obsessed with our flaws and ultimately hindering ourselves from the blessings of God.

Granted, we need to be nurtured. Yes, we need to be loved. But more than anything, singles need to awake to the call God has on their life! We have so much potential with our time but often carelessly let the days slip through our fingers waiting, pining, hoping, and praying . . . anything but acting. God's Word clearly states that single believers were crucial to impacting the world for Christ in the early church. I will be a modern-day Paul if that is what God calls me to be. I will drop my nets to follow Him. Want to walk on water? Be like Peter and get out of the boat. I want to see and do miracles in His name. What do you want to do? Another "bigger and better" treasure hunt in your single adults class, or do you want to actually change someone's life in the process of changing yours?

Life is similar to investments. You can buy a new home or you can buy a new car. Which asset is more likely to produce a rising value in the future? Since homes (for the most part) appreciate and cars depreciate, wouldn't it be wiser to put your money into a home where the value will continue to grow? How do you devote your life? Do you hold investments in Christ or does the world hold your savings account? Matthew 6:19–21 says, "Do not store up for yourselves treasure on earth, where moth and rust destroy, and where thieves break in and steal. But store up for yourselves treasures in heaven, where moth and rust do not destroy, and where thieves do not break in and steal. For where your treasure is, there your heart will be also" (NIV). I can tell you that I have an account with the First National Bank of God that is drawing interest even as I write this. What treasure chest are you filling? What drives you?

THE END OF OURSELVES

Michelle and I have both traveled the world ministering. No matter where we go, the most popular question is always: How do you deal with loneliness? To be perfectly honest, we are so crazy busy and in love with Christ, we really don't have time to be lonely too often. My schedule screams for my presence somewhere all the time, so I've long since traded in that particular burden. But since I have come out the other side, let me tell you what I've learned. Stop for a second and ponder this . . . Could it be the loneliness that plagues you is not a curse but a blessing in disguise? I'm regularly battered by the circumstances of my life; isn't everyone? But I'm not any worse for the wear. I'm from the camp that whatever doesn't kill us makes us stronger. Oh, there will always be the other times, when it is all you can do to remain tearless before you hit your driveway. You'll stumble in the door, drop the mail on the floor, and collapse on the couch longing for someone, anyone, to put their arms around you and tell you it's all right. On those rare occasions for me, a hot bath, a cup of tea, and a long-overdue cry will fix me up for another year. (I'm fairly confident that it's a hormone thing.) However, if you struggle with loneliness constantly, it's time to reexamine your priorities. Find the root of your unhappiness; discover your purpose. If you have a bout once a month, you're what I would consider actively living in the happy medium. No matter how hard we try not to let it bother us, loneliness can still get the best of us occasionally. When you do fall prey to the emotions, try my solution above. If that doesn't work, resolve yourself to a bad day, but consciously start fresh the next morning. If you can't get over the hurdle and one bad day rolls into ten, it's possible that you may even have a case of clinical depression, which would be better treated with medication and professional counseling. Don't rule out your body's ability to run your emotions!

So I can guess what you're thinking: *How can all the battle scars that flaunt our loneliness be considered a good thing?* It's a pretty simple theory, really. On the days we are the "masters of our universe," we quite frankly don't "need" the Lord as much. We may throw out some genuine and sincere praises to Him here or there, but our level of dependence is significantly higher on days where nothing is going right. So can we for the sake of argument assume, then, that bad days (weeks, months, years, too) could actually be considered a good thing? In those weak moments, where we reach the end of ourselves, isn't that where we finally run to God? Some cling to Him faithfully no matter what, but when times are tough, isn't that when, like David, we cry out and finally place our broken hearts in His hands to reshape? Or could you find yourself playing on the team that runs from the issue? "God doesn't love me" has become your cry. The tape "Surely He has abandoned me. If He could see what goes on in my house, He would fix my life; therefore, He simply must not care" is what has been recorded and constantly replays in your mind. But let's take a step back and look at the bigger picture. God says He will never leave us nor forsake us, and we essentially have to take Him at His word.

Generally, we don't talk to God until we need to, and it's pretty curious how, at the first sign of trouble, we instantly start replaying in our mind all those missed appointments—all the times we skipped church, forgot our daily time with Him, or dodged His promptings. But when we are walking with Him, we know He's still there, and we quickly get past our embarrassment of slighting Him.

Max Lucado has said that "loneliness is not the absence of faces. It is the absence of intimacy." How do tired, beat-up, lonely people who so desperately need intimacy get their fill? Singles have the preconceived notion that it's found in a mate. Married people think it's found in solitude. In 1969, the band Three Dog Night rode to fame on the song "One" written by Harry Nilsson. Society as a whole embraced the tune, driving it to the number five slot on the pop charts that year. Lyrically, the song is about as depressing as it gets: "One is the loneliest number that there ever was. Two can be as bad as one, it's the loneliest number since the number one." I feel that I can safely assume since "two can be as bad as one," a mate isn't necessarily the answer. Some of you are thinking, *But having a mate is surely better than being alone.*

First, let's clarify: Being alone is one thing, being lonely is completely different. Since I am with people a majority of the time, I've discovered it's very easy to find people with like interests and goals, people to "hang out" with. I am rarely ever alone. However, when it comes down to sharing deep, dark secrets with someone you can trust, it is a completely different story. We can have constant companionship but be unsatisfied with the level of intimacy those relationships offer.

DISCOVERY 101

I was able to face my loneliness head-on several years ago. Well before my days of full-time ministry, I worked long hours in health care, made too much money for someone of my age, but rarely had the chance to be lonely. Despite the fact that I was making a very good salary and had plenty of friends (even some dates!), I was still unsatisfied with my life. I began to seek a way to become truly happy. Yes, I had a great church, nice things, good friends, and a relationship with Christ. I had a cool apartment, a decent vehicle, and money, but some dimension was missing.

I discovered that somewhere along the line I'd stopped depending on God. I thought I had become self-sufficient and I stopped seeking Him for my basic needs. I took breathing, eating, living, and loving for granted. I was lonely because I'd moved away from God. I grew content in my own abilities and my own strength. Upon realization of that (and the Lord's leading me into full-time ministry working with artists), I resigned from my comfy, well-paying job and jumped off the bridge into trust. (My salary dropped by 84 percent . . . You can't convince me that wasn't done on faith.) When I was no longer under the illusion that I was self-sufficient and was looking at maintaining a pretty comfortable standard of living even without the hefty paychecks, I quickly returned to my senses. I realized I had never actually been self-sufficient and departed from my prideful mind-set, once again finding my contentment and happiness based in the Lord's providing for me, not in my ability to provide for myself.

I spend many nights in complete solitude, happy to be away from the masses. I am very content with my lone existence in those moments of silence (since they are so rare). Occasionally, there are times when I'm not so thrilled with my lot. Generally, it's after a hard weekend on the road that I'm ticked because my man hasn't found me yet to release me from *his* curse (You get to work, honey; I'll have the babies. That's the deal in Genesis 3). When loneliness sets in (for anyone), it is because there is a natural need that is not being met. We have isolated ourselves either from God or from others. We have to have a healthy balance of both in our lives. It is in my loneliness, however, that my heart cries out to my Creator.

GET YOUR HOUSE IN ORDER

Don't doubt the call; we *all* have the same task: *Go!* "Go therefore and make disciples of all the nations, baptizing them in the name of the Father and of the Son and of the Holy Spirit, teaching them to observe all things that I have commanded you; and lo, I am with you always, even to the end of the age" (Matt. 28:19–20 NKJV). So, how we do we walk from being called to being committed singles?

Do you know His voice? Are you listening? "(Now Samuel did not yet know the LORD, nor was the word of the LORD yet revealed to him.) And the LORD called Samuel again the third time. So he arose and went to Eli, and said, 'Here I am, for you did call me.' Then Eli perceived that the LORD had called the boy" (1 Sam. 3:7–8 NKJV). Three calls later, Eli finally figured it out—it was the Lord calling Samuel. Have you been assuming that voice inside is coming from your own little Jiminy Cricket? Listen again; it just might be the Lord. Can you truthfully and willingly answer, "Speak, for Your servant hears"? Better yet, are you willing to act on what He tells you?

You have to sit at His feet. (You know . . . "Be still, and know that I am God" [Ps. 46:10 NKJV].) Run to any place where you can sit in His presence without distraction. I don't care if you go to your backyard, a closet, or Starbuck's, but make the time to be with Him, free of distractions. If it helps you to sit in your car and talk into your cell phone, put a pretend speed dial to God on there! Whatever it takes; if you want to be a satisfied single, you have to make the commitment to get intimate with Jesus! If you make a point of it, He will meet you and will be faithful to reveal His plans for you. "Commit your works to the LORD, and your thoughts will be established" (Prov. 16:3 NKJV).

If you're really serious about turning your weakness into strength, take one hour a day and turn off the television, the radio, and all the junk that corrodes minds and morals . . . and dwell on Christ. "Finally, brethren, whatever things are true, whatever things are noble, whatever things are just, whatever things are pure, whatever things are lovely, whatever things are of good report, if there is any virtue and if there is anything praiseworthy—meditate on these things. The things which you learned and received and heard and saw in me, these do, and the God of peace will be with you" (Phil. 4:8–9 NKJV).

Sitcoms, R-rated movies, and Howard Stern radio programs don't qualify for true, pure, or lovely. I'm preaching to the choir here (I can always make better choices), but turn off the trash! Garbage in, garbage out. "For out of the abundance of the heart the mouth speaks" (Matt. 12:34 NKJV). If your schedule is already full without those distractions, wake up early or stay awake an hour later to dedicate some time to just sitting at His feet in study. Get in His Word and hide it in your heart!

PAYING YOUR DUES

Tithe! "Will a man rob God? Yet you have robbed Me! But you say, 'In what way have we robbed You?' In tithes and offerings. You are cursed with a curse, for you have robbed Me, even this whole nation" (Mal. 3:8–9 NKJV). *Friend, do not cheat here!* I know as singles we have one income, and it's certainly more cost-effective to have more people in the household to contribute to the bills. When you don't, the budget is tight; I understand. You will, however, shoot yourself in the foot by ignoring this statute. One hundred percent of what you have is the Lord's. He's only asking you for one-tenth of it. Do not lose blessings because you need to pay your electric or credit-card bills! Some of us foolishly sacrifice blessings because we'd rather have a new pair of shoes or go on an impulsive trip with the girls.

When you get your paycheck, the very first check you write should be to your local church where you are fed and worship. (Do not send your tithes to other national ministries such as mine or television; those gifts are considered offerings.) When I get paid, I write the tithe check immediately so that I offer first-fruits to the Lord (and so I don't forget). I will tell you that there are months when it appears I will be short in meeting all the demands of life. But I write His requested portion of the funds in faith, knowing that my needs will be met. I have yet to go hungry and have never had my lights cut off.

Let's say you make four hundred dollars a week. You have eighty-five dollars left and still two weeks before your next payday. There are groceries yet to buy and the water bill still to pay, and who even knows what else can come up between now and then. You forgot to pay your tithe off the top (which at eighty dollars even, would leave you just five). What do you do? Write the check to the Lord. I dare you to be obedient. I beg you to be obedient. You cannot outgive God. Read further in Malachi:

> "Bring all the tithes into the storehouse, that there may be food in My house, and try Me now in this," says the LORD of hosts, "if I will not open for you the windows of heaven and pour out for you such blessing that there will not be room enough to receive it. And I will rebuke the devourer for your sakes, so that he will not destroy the fruit of your ground, nor shall the vine fail to bear fruit for you in the field." (Mal. 3:10–11 NKJV)

I think that tithing is imperative for any Christian, especially those preparing for service. We need to be ready to do the work of the Lord, and this is one area that prepares the ground. "Aaron is to present the Levites before the LORD as a wave offering from the Israelites, so that they may be ready to do the work of the LORD" (Num. 8:11 NIV). God will supply all your needs, but be wise in this area, and God will be faithful! Try the Lord and see if you can outgive Him!

Finally, work for the Lord, not for friends, family, or anyone else. He is the One calling the shots and calling you. No matter what task He gives you, give it all your effort. "And whatever you do, do it heartily, as to the Lord and not to men" (Col. 3:23 NKJV). Work hard for the right reason. Advances, bonuses, and commissions are all just gravy in the grand scheme. God will equip you through the power of His Word. Be "confident of this, that he who began a good work in you will carry it on to completion until the day of Christ Jesus" (Phil. 1:6 NIV).

I have a friend who thrives on instant gratification. She graciously mowed my yard on several occasions just to achieve a sense of accomplishment. (I can personally get the same exhilaration by calling my lawn man, but to each his own, right?) I, too, can get in the mind-set that if it doesn't have an instant payoff, if I can't see the end of the line, then I won't make time for it in my life. Don't limit God by not following through with His desires. He doesn't need you; He chose you, and His time frame is not yours. Do not be frustrated if you are planting seeds and not reaping great harvests! God is busy preparing the way and needs some to plant, some to water, and some to reap. Be faithful in those divine appointments, no matter what your role!

Finally, the words of Paul are my greatest comfort when I am weak from carrying the cross:

> But whatever was to my profit I now consider loss for the sake of Christ. What is more, I consider everything a loss compared to the surpassing greatness of knowing Christ Jesus my Lord, for whose sake I have lost all things. I consider them rubbish, that I may gain Christ and be found in him, not having a righteousness of my own that comes from the law, but that which is through faith in Christ—the righteousness that comes from God and is by faith. I want to know Christ and the power of his resurrection and the fellowship of sharing in his sufferings. (Phil. 3:7–10 NIV)

Fellow single, grip grace, cling to comfort, hold on to hope. It's true that two are better than one. But, if you are willing, you can do anything with God. "For when I am weak, then I am strong" (2 Cor. 12:10 NIV).

ℰ

Oooh, girl, why do you want to be so hard on a sister? Sometimes, once you've made it over the hill it's hard to remember what the valley looked like, but I'm going to try to break down where you were coming from a little bit more.

What can be said about why and how we crave what we crave? It's amazing that we can raid the refrigerator looking for something to satisfy us, eat everything in sight, and still feel unsatisfied. So many times we mistake spiritual hunger for physical or emotional hunger. We need this, we crave that . . . Most of the time, all we need is a really good session with the Lover of our soul. He says in Isaiah 55:2–3, "Why spend money on what is not bread, and your labor on what does not satisfy? Listen, listen to me, and eat what is good, and your soul will delight in the richest of fare. Give ear and come to me; hear me, that your soul may live. I will make an everlasting covenant with you, my faithful love promised to David" (NIV). There it is. Even God knew we were hungry for the wrong thing and promised us love instead. Could it be that we are trying to fill up on all the wrong things, the wrong type of love from the wrong men, the wrong type of baubles and material possessions, in order to fill a place in our heart that is not shaped to receive anything other than God Himself?

ENDLESS SURPRISES

I am continually fascinated when I consider how Adam must have spent his time in the garden before Eve came along. What *did* he do in that garden all day? There was no hard work to distract him, the earth watered itself. Everything grew decently and in order. There wasn't really anything to do. Though he was busy supervising God's creation, this was not taxing work. God showed up for evening walks, but what did Adam do in the meantime? Perhaps those conversations filled him up so that all he could do the next day was lie around and think about what God had said. Some sermons have left me feeling like that. Truly, man does not live by bread alone but by every word that proceeds from the mouth of God.

But that is exactly what we are afraid of—what will proceed from God's mouth. Heaven forbid that He magnify our faults any bigger than they already are in our eyes or that we have to change something! That would be just too much like real work. And how about the fact that if we really got close to Him, He might start to rearrange our plans? You know we don't really trust Him with our future. After all, He might turn us all into missionaries and send us to minister to naked people somewhere and leave all our jewelry and makeup at home. I don't *want* to be peculiar; I just want to be normal and have a basically predictable life like everyone else around me who has a husband, two kids, and a dog . . . Wait a minute! What am I saying? I could never be that consistently domestic. I much prefer the life of endless surprises I have with God. He is the most exciting Man I know. As for being peculiar, well if I'm truly honest, I was that way before I came to Christ.

GETTING TO KNOW HIM

We have all these weird ideas about what being intimate with God will do to us because we don't really know Him. We assume that He isn't as good as everyone says He is. I dare you to find out that He is. I challenge you to open your Bible and read it as if you are reading *People* magazine. I bet you know more about Hugh Grant and John Travolta than you do about God. That is pitiful; it's time to get up on the Word. Don't worry about all the "Thou shalt nots," just decide to find out everything about this Man who is the Lover of your soul. The bottom line is, do you know enough about Him to have any sort of interesting conversation with Him?

Yes, your love life will affect your prayer life, your passion for sharing Christ with others, your giving (Holly beat you up enough about that, so I'm gonna leave it alone except to second the motion) . . . You know the drill, all the things He asks us to do. Small wonder He said that if we love Him with all our heart, our soul, our mind, and our strength, the rest will fall into place. The commandments will be covered, because if we love Him, we will keep His commandments.

Think about when you've fallen in love in the past. Think of all the changes you made to be one with the person you were so cra-aa-zy about. Uh-huh, now you see what I'm talking about. Get out of your head and into your heart when it comes to having a love affair with God. It can be all-consuming and fulfilling if you let it. And . . . it will make you much more discerning in your mate selection, because you'll already be feeling the love. There will be no propensity toward desperate, foolish moves. Your love cup will already be full. You will not tolerate anything less than what you are experiencing already. Anyone who detracts from the peace you now know will have to go. Take it from me. There is such a thing as being happy alone.

11 The Frustration Factor

I cried out to the LORD because of my affliction, and He answered me.

—JONAH 2:2 NKJV

I just spent two hours trying to find someone, anyone, to help me take my car to the repair shop. My original plan of a friend helping me flew out the window. So she's not the most reliable person in the world . . . groan. After a similar ordeal earlier in the summer, I spent six hours waiting in the stale gray waiting room of the greasy auto-repair shop and ended up spending a few hundred bucks for a tune-up, transmission flush, oil change, and fuel filter replacement. It was a little pre-sixty-thousand-mile treat. I thought it would spruce up the performance of my vehicle and help me out on its fuel consumption. When I got it back, it ran worse than it did when I took it in, and my mileage dropped to a mere six miles a gallon. Okay, that's a problem.

Well, I assumed it would eventually get better since the first couple of tanks after a tune-up are generally pretty poor, right? However, since I travel via planes mostly, I haven't driven too terribly much this summer. And since trying to get your vehicle to the shop when you're single is about as easy as finding a four-leaf clover in Arizona, I always put it off until absolutely necessary. My schedule has been so hectic, I pretty much have just given in to having normal maintenance-type things like getting the oil changed or tires rotated done by my parking company while I'm away on a trip.

Of course, my "regular" mechanic is probably about as honest as Benedict Arnold. He's cute, but I don't trust him any farther than I can throw him. I have some invalidated fears relating to sabotage in light of the fact that my daddy lives five hundred miles away and I have no real protector on hand to accompany me to the den of auto deceit. I know my service writer thinks I'm ignorant of automotive rhetoric, undoubtedly because I'm a girl, and I agree to and regularly pay too much money for services I probably don't even need. As a result, lately I've been trying to call my dad or one of my guy friends so I can at least have some kind of spark plug mumbo jumbo to rattle off. On my trip to the shop this afternoon to complain about my gas consumption problem, he informed me that he wants to run a diagnostic test, which is a fancy way for him to say it'll cost me to find out what's wrong and cost me to fix what they find. It's a shame he's so adorable. Makes me less willing to put up a fight, ya know? (Note: He is a "cute" heathen, so the whole being hot thing is pretty much a moot issue until I can get the boy to Jesus. Aw, shucks.)

Even though he's "fine," I'd still be avoiding taking it to the shop if I didn't have a road trip coming up. Who has time for such inconveniences? I have a deadline, a boss who needs things done, and a huge urge to move to the Caribbean to set up a dive shop.

I've worked about seventy-five hours this week and won't be here next. So no, I don't have time to take my car to the mechanic, and I certainly don't want to spend any more money. However, I can't drive a thousand miles with it running like a rat trap!

So I find myself sitting outside my "friend's" apartment after midnight with no "friend" in sight. After twenty minutes and no show, I head back toward the shop. It's only two little miles from my house. I'd already considered tossing my bike into the back of the Explorer to just ride home; however, when I tried to implement that plan, I discovered the bike had two flat tires. No problem, I have a handy new bike pump right here, still in its original packaging. (I love it when I'm McGyverish.) Only the new pump I bought, well, it doesn't actually work; something is sliding around in there and it isn't pumping any air. Isn't that lovely. Back to square one—one body, one car, and two miles separating point A from point B.

At this juncture, I'm tempted to just leave the thing here and walk home . . . only it's well past midnight. That is probably not the safest or wisest choice available. I'd do it, only the two miles is uphill the whole way! I did want to sleep at some point tonight. Oh yes, it's so grand to be single.

SUCH IS LIFE

I can't tell you how often scenarios like that come up. You know and could add a few of your own, I'm sure. I'm sitting here writing this . . . still trying to figure out a way to get my car in to be worked on and, frankly, I'm just frustrated that I don't have a sweet little hubby who would run down there with me, drop off the suffering vehicle, set the cocky and condescending mechanic straight, and come jump in the car with me to live happily ever after. Is that so much to ask? Why in the world can't it be that easy for us singles? Maybe I don't need a husband, maybe just an unlimited bank account would work?

Honestly, that's just the tip of the iceberg when it comes to things I'm frustrated about. I'm irked at how unfair it seems that despite my skills in cooking, cleaning, sewing, and serving, I haven't found anyone to take me to the dumb mechanic's. I'm not asking for much! After all, it's not like I'm asking Him to make me thin, just get me a good guy. I have these "issues" with the Lord, mostly surrounding the fact that I've been faithfully boning up on my Proverbs 31 guidelines to be this great wife and mother, and I live alone with a cat and a perfectly good car that a mechanic keeps wreaking havoc on because he can. (In the grand scheme, at least his delightful presence is a plus.) Great . . . I'm never getting married.

There has to be some answer I'm missing here. In my present state, I'm reminded of Jonah. From the world's point of view, Jonah and the whale have become a part of literature, a part of the mythology archive. It's construed as little more than an exaggerated fish tale. However, it's not a fable, it's a story about one reluctant prophet who just couldn't quite get it right. Jonah had his own set of "issues." My life always falls into better perspective after I study this short book in the Minor Prophets.

Most everyone knows the basics about how God called Jonah to go and preach to the people of Nineveh, and how he hopped on a boat heading the opposite direction because he didn't want to go and preach to those heathens. Then the big storm came up, scared the crew to death, and they tossed him overboard. Of course, the climax of the story is familiar: Jonah lives through the harrowing experience of being swallowed alive by a fish and spending days in fishy digestive juices. Once Jonah realized his desperate situation and how his disobedience took him there, he called out to the Lord.

Since the Lord still needed someone to go to Ninevah, and it seemed Jonah had turned the corner as far as his attitude, he was seemingly "rescued" by being spit out (I used nice words there) onto dry land and finally got around to doing what he was originally supposed to do. Clap, clap, yea, yea. Good job, Jonah! Most of our knowledge of Jonah ends where the Sunday school flannel graph ends. However, there is much more to this prophet's rating than the positive review we've given him all these years.

GIVING UP AND GIVING IN

Jonah 3 shows our wayward man finally doing what God intended him to do. This reluctant prophet is being a vehicle of God's grace, preaching to those disgusting Ninevites. Ordinarily, that kind of message wouldn't have gotten much of a response. There are reports in the Bible that other prophets were sent with a message like this, and no one paid attention to it. But an amazing thing happens in Nineveh this time . . . they listen. "So the people of Nineveh believed God, proclaimed a fast, and put on sackcloth, from the greatest to the least of them" (Jonah 3:5 NKJV). And when the king heard about it,

> he arose from his throne and laid aside his robe, covered himself with sackcloth and sat in ashes. And he caused it to be proclaimed and published throughout Nineveh by the decree of the king and his nobles, saying, Let neither man nor beast, herd nor flock, taste anything; do not let them eat, or drink water. But let man and beast be covered with sackcloth, and cry mightily to God; yes, let every one turn from his evil way and from the violence that is in his hands. (Jonah 3:6–8 NKJV)

This city was spared! But why did they listen to Jonah's message but not to the other prophets'? I would consider it a mystery we won't have the exact answer to until heaven; however, we might have a little insight from the Gospel of Luke: "For as Jonah became a sign to the Ninevites, so also the Son of Man will be to this generation" (11:30 NKJV). I sometimes wonder if it was the fishy scent he wore—"Eau de Fish Belly" splash-on? There are also reports of others surviving and their skin turning a chalky white from the digestive juices. So, we are left to ponder if it was his appearance that made him a "sign."

But now jump to chapter 4. Here is where we get back into some grit. It's here that his true character is fully revealed. Right off the bat we find the "holy man" beside himself with anger that they responded to the Lord's message and became saved! Huh? Wasn't that his whole job as a prophet? Jonah 3:10 says that the Lord God "had compassion and did not bring upon them [the Ninevites] the destruction he had threatened" (NIV). Yet look again at what Jonah 4:1 tells us: "But Jonah was greatly displeased and became angry" (NIV). This verse is actually translated from the Hebrew to read, "But it was a *very evil* thing to Jonah."

The wording here is harsh, no-holds-barred language. Jonah wasn't just disgruntled with God—he was livid! Grasp the seriousness of this accusation. Jonah is calling God evil. (Lightning rods up!) If I were God, I'd flick Jonah's trifling little head back to Joppa and be done with him! (See why God hasn't given me any kids yet?)

WAITING FOR THE SHOE TO DROP

But it gets even worse. Jonah then pouts about it! Call me a big chicken, but I hope I never get to the point that I tell the Lord He can just take my life because it's better for me to die than to live. All because someone I didn't like found Him? How sad is the fact that this "man of God" stomped off to a corner to pout? But that's exactly what he did. "So Jonah went out of the city and sat on the east side of the city. There he made himself a shelter and sat under it in the shade, till he might see what would become of the city" (Jonah 4:5 NKJV). Apparently, Jonah was convinced that their newfound "religion" wasn't too sincere, so he camped out to watch their impending demise. It's ironic how the coin has flipped—God now offering grace, and Jonah holding out for destruction.

If we pause to evaluate it, we see why Jonah left for Tarshish in the first place. He knew the Lord would be compassionate and merciful, and he didn't want that for these people! His pride is damaged—he's fuming mad—and all he knows to do is give up. It's just not fair that God is so gracious! Conversely, this little glimpse of his heart brings up vivid images of this tattered, fish-slobbery prophet walking through Nineveh with the greatest message in the world. Can't you just see him being less than enthusiastic, basically just going through the motions? His apathy for their souls had to come through in his delivery, wouldn't you think? Listen to his voice monotonously saying, "Yet forty days, and Nineveh shall be overthrown." Some sort of Charlie Brown's teacher type *"waaa waa waa waa"* speaking after that. I can't see him excited about it, that's for sure.

But back to the facts. The Lord is about to educate Jonah in value placement. In Jonah 4:6–8, God "provides" on three separate occasions. The Lord provided a leafy plant to cover Jonah so he would be protected from the sun; a worm to eat the plant, causing it to die; and then a scorching east wind to make Jonah uncomfortable. It's interesting that the word used here for "scorching east wind" is *sirocco*. The same word is used in the book of Job to describe the powerful east wind that blew down the walls of the homes of Job's children. This leads me to believe that God means business and will put forth every effort to make His point.

DIVINE PROVIDENCE

Regardless, this act of provision by God is an example of where we get the theological doctrine of the providence of God. God's providence essentially implies that God intervenes in the everyday affairs of mankind to bring about His desired plans. In this particular instance, God bestowed these three things to teach Jonah a lesson—to teach *us* a lesson.

Anyway, God prepared the plant, and we see in verse 6 that Jonah was grateful for it, and then parts two and three of the lesson go into effect. Notice the calculated details here. God appointed, or prepared, an east wind that blew the heat of the desert in upon Jonah; and the whining prophet sat there in the sweltering heat until he fainted and asked that he might die (is your imagery dragging up that of a big baby?). The God of second chances asked of him again, "Is it right for you to be angry about the plant?" (Jonah 4:9 NKJV). Jonah has a fighting chance here, and I am amazed at how stubborn this prophet was. You can just hear his little-boy reply, which also serves as his last recorded words: "It is right for me to be angry, even to death" (v. 9 NKJV). (He is way too high-maintenance for me at this point. Flick!) Poor God; Jonah did it, and I know we do, too. (Hey, don't flick me God!)

I find it all too familiar that as long as things are going well for Jonah he is content with the Lord, but when things don't go as he thought they would, he gets mad. How do you react to the Lord when things don't work out as you had hoped or planned? I don't know about you, but I fall prey to my own wants and desires and can get a little cranky myself at times. But I do know that I sure don't want my last words on record to be "back talk" to the Lord. Know what I mean?

God's point to Jonah is that Jonah had nothing to do with the plant growing or dying, yet he cared so much more for that silly little plant. However, he was upset that God cared for the people of Nineveh, whom God had created. You know, it's natural to point the finger at Jonah, but haven't you ever laid it out and said, "I want what I want when I want it. I don't care what You do as long as You do it now. I don't like the way You're running things. Take me away to heaven!"?

Listen to the Lord's tender admonishment to Jonah:

> You pity the plant, for which you did not labor, nor did you make it grow, which came into being in a night, and perished in a night. And should not I pity Nineveh, that great city, in which there are more than a hundred and twenty thousand persons who do not know their right hand from their left? (Jonah 4:10–11 RSV)

Frankly, I'm a little astonished that the God of the universe would care enough to pause here in the midst of His busy schedule (I would think there would be lots of "paperwork" since Nineveh was getting written into the Lamb's book of life hand over fist!) to try to explain His ways to some unruly child. What a picture of His care and concern for us.

This little four-chapter book doesn't end all neat and tidy as we'd like it to. In fact, it's quite far from it. We are left on the edge of the proverbial cliff by the final words of God to Jonah, words of rebuke. We are never told that Jonah apologized or made things right. I'm not sure why it ends so sadly or abruptly, but it could be for many reasons. Personally, I believe it's because there is no final solution to the sin of self-righteousness or the mentality that we deserve the good things we get. Therefore, I think the conclusion is fitting, leaving us a little off balance and with lots to ponder. But poor Jonah, I hope he came around again.

LOOKING IN THE MIRROR

Then again, not only did Jonah typify the spiritual state of Israel in his own day, he also prototyped the self-righteousness (if we were honest) that you and I struggle with. Unfortunately, rejecting the grace, mercy, and sovereignty of God is just as customary a sin today as it was in Jonah's time. We become frustrated with our situation as well as with God, for the same erroneous reasons as Jonah. We just don't have a guy running around with a quill and parchment to record our stupidity. *Oh, I never do that,* you might be thinking. I imagine that self-righteousness has deeply penetrated our lives, and we aren't even aware of it most of the time. Consider that we have become a people exceedingly likely to take credit for our own successes and prosperity.

As a whole we have come to accept as fact that we have been "blessed" due to our own intelligence, ingenuity, and hard work, and our service and devotion to God have caused Him to bless us. Our works-based mentality doesn't change reality, however. We expect or think we deserve something from God and become frustrated or angry when He doesn't give it to us. When we come to the mind-set that someone else is unworthy, we are angry with God for giving them blessings we feel they don't deserve. When our blessings stop flowing, we think He has no right to remove them.

Let's remember that God's grace does not always come in the form we might choose or prefer. God was exceedingly gracious to save Jonah by means of the great fish. However, had Jonah been able to choose which form the grace of God would take, it probably wouldn't have been his first choice to end up in that fish's belly.

THE GOOD, THE BAD, AND THE UGLY

Job understood that God was both good and gracious, whether He gave prosperity or took it away, whether He gave pleasure or pain. Thus, when he was delivered the news regarding the loss of his family he responded, "The LORD gave, and the LORD has taken away; blessed be the name of the LORD" (Job 1:21 NKJV).

Oh, I know that I have little to do with the circumstance of singleness in my life. I'm certainly not a write-off. I'm fun, a nice person (most of the time), and I'm not addicted to anything (bad), so I might have a fighting chance if I ever get to spend a few days in the same zip code. But for now, I know I just need to hold tight to the truths and lessons He's personally walked me through already. Trials, suffering, and all forms of adversity are often the result of God's grace, because when these things come into the life of the believer, they should display the grace of God, not send us into pouty tantrums like Jonah.

Just like today at the mechanic's. I woke up early (too early for the one Saturday I was actually home), gave my frustration for the whole ordeal over to the Lord, and schlepped my smiling face down to the garage where I knew I'd be firmly planted for a few hours. I spent the whole morning there in the same stale, gray, greasy customer waiting area with strangers. Oh, I certainly could have better utilized my time elsewhere, but I took a book and rested in His provision for the day. So you know what? I may be single, and while it takes a small act of God for me to get my car to the service station, I know He's still in control.

He has His own way of showing me He knows, and I just need to hang on to Him . . . that my frustration is all an act of futility. How do I know? Who else gets free mechanic service in addition to a complimentary oil change by a commissions-based service writer when they are a "dumb" girl, with an oversized trendy vehicle that happens to be getting cruddy gas mileage? Me, that's who, just this morning! This single girl has a Fiancé who owns the cattle on a thousand hills and has an inside track to that (cute) service writer's heart and mind. The way I look at it, when the FOG (favor of God) rolls in, it has a much better effect than if my earthly husband took in the car. After all, we'd be out a hundred and fifty bucks then!

❧

Jonah, Jonah, Jonah—don't be too hard on him, Miss Holly. I can relate! When you've been being a good little Christian it's easy to feel that God should spank all the bad children. But that's where the danger is, isn't it? After all, what is so good about you? How do you know you're that good? Whose measuring stick are you using? You could be doing all the right things on the outside and have a mind like a toilet. Jesus said as much about the Pharisees; He said they looked fabulous on the outside, but inside they were sepulchers. In Matthew 23:27, He calls them whitewashed tombs. He wasn't too happy with them, though they seemed to be very happy with themselves. In 1 Corinthians 3:18, we are warned not to think too highly of ourselves, lest we become deceived and fall. Ooooh! I've been there. Looking down my self-righteous nose at those who were in sexual sin or doing something else stupid and not dealing with the fact that perhaps the Lord was looking at my eating or spending habits in the same light. I hope I'm not hurting too many people here, but that's the bottom line: We all pick an area to abuse as compensation for what we think God hasn't yet provided in our lives.

RELEASING THE IDOLS

I've got to revisit Jonah's profound statement after he got all that seaweed unwrapped from around his head: "I've realized that those who cling to worthless idols forfeit the grace that could be theirs." This is one of my favorite Scriptures because it pretty much sums up our attitude toward life. As I've mentioned before it took Jonah three days to say something God wanted to hear. Now, that's me talking.

The Scripture actually says that Jonah prayed on the third day. I personally don't believe it took Jonah three days to pray. I think he spent the first two days pontificating and telling God what He should do and God waited until he got a grip on himself. Telling God what to do is like standing completely naked with no purse or wallet outside the locked doors of Saks Fifth Avenue and demanding they open the store and give you something to wear. Why would they? You look a little crazy, plus, you obviously have no money to pay for anything. So who's in power here? How do you tell the Creator of the universe what to do, even if you *are* talking about your life? Remember, He created you, too.

Those who cling to worthless idols . . . Be honest about what worthless idols those might be. How about the way you think your life should go? Your overwhelming desire to be married? Your career? Your obsession with your body or material things? It's pretty much anything that exalts itself above the knowledge of God's love and His will for your life. Anything that robs you of your contentment. Because lack of contentment means that you have moved God off the throne of your heart and chosen to independently pursue pleasure by your own means.

Let's face it. Some of us are evil with God because we're secretly jealous that all those other folks seem to be having fun and we're not. If that is really where you are, you need to examine that. Why does what they are doing look good to you? If you truly love God, you will love what He loves and hate what He hates. Through His eyes, sin doesn't look so good, it's a turnoff, it makes you go, "Yuck!" Downright distasteful. The fruit of the Spirit tastes so much better. However, if you insist on harboring backward glances at those playing in the dark, God will sit with you for a time and even cover you as you muse about what "those" folk out there are getting away with. But if you don't hurry up and get over it, He will allow you to be overwhelmed by the heat of your inner dissatisfaction until you long to die—to yourself.

The scary part is, God will leave you to deal with yourself. He will allow you to become uncomfortable. You know, that itchy, awful place where you grow sick and tired of being sick and tired and you're finally ready to listen to reason.

Then God softly comes to reason with us. We can either have the sense to admit He is right and knows best or we can continue to argue and grow more uncomfortable. It's up to us. The bottom line is, we *don't know* what's best for us. We are silly little sheep. We sheep need a Shepherd to lead us to safe ground, to pastures that will supply all we need. And when it's time to switch pastures, well, He'll take care of that, too.

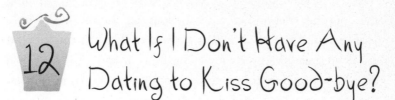

12 What If I Don't Have Any Dating to Kiss Good-bye?

*Here is my servant, whom I uphold, my chosen one in whom
I delight; I will put my Spirit on him and he will bring justice to the nations.*

—ISAIAH 42:1 NIV

Every person who maintains the single life for any length of
time will undoubtedly be asked, "Are you dating anyone?" and
"Why aren't you married yet?" Lately, instead of pretending I'm
not ticked by those thoughtless questions, I lamely respond with
something to place blame on, such as my college experience, and
retreat from the conversation to find someone more courteous
to talk with. It enrages me because I can't help but think they
are rather ignorant. Anyone who knows me surely would agree
that if I knew why I'm single . . . if I were *in the know* . . . I
wouldn't be in this situation. Hello? Is there a class people take
on the torture of singles?

No, I'm not dating anyone currently; in fact, I bought some
stock in *I Kissed Dating Good-bye* (by Joshua Harris). So get off

my back, Jack! Of course, truth be told, I haven't intentionally kissed dating good-bye. It kind of fell by the wayside all on its own. However, I think there is a lot to be said for approaching the courting relationship with wisdom and humility. The only problem with the book is that there are Christian singles who are discouraged because they've never even had a shot at a real date. How do you kiss something good-bye you don't have? What happens when you find yourself on some non-self-imposed dating fast? What's the nondating Christian single to do?

Well, they say the path of discovery leads to self. Honestly, many people never date because of their lack of self-esteem or poor self-image. Sadly enough, we have missed the boat on the end of Romans 13:9, which says we are to love our neighbors as we love ourselves. Unfortunately, there are some of us who can't follow through with loving others because we don't even like ourselves. Biblically, the whole love thing is pretty clear: "Though I speak with the tongues of men and of angels, but have not love, I have become sounding brass or a clanging cymbal" (1 Cor. 13:1 NKJV). Having a problem loving yourself? Ask God to help you see yourself as He sees you. Find your worth, value, and love in Him. Bathe yourself in Scripture that will infuse your soul with His worth and His value and His Love for you. He is faithful to give to those who ask. When you see yourself through His eyes, your entire world will be turned upside down.

REBEL WITHOUT A CLUE

Some don't date because of mere circumstances. (Oooh! Oooh! Can I blame mine on that?) My choice of colleges was very comparable to a military boot camp (which I didn't realize until after I enrolled). I was very fortunate to attend a beautiful private Christian college located in Florida, and despite my story, really have no regrets (well, other than wishing I had made it to the beach a little more often).

After reading through the brochures (and growing up in farmlandville, Illinois), I was pretty sure my dorm room would have a sliding glass door that opened right onto the beach. In preparation for my starry-eyed trip to college, I bought myself a new King James Version Bible (the required translation) and was careful not to have my name imprinted on it, so when I married I wouldn't waste a perfectly good Bible. I also acquired a whole new wardrobe of dresses, skirts, culottes ("shorts" that looked like mini tents), and a drawer full of hosiery (yes, in Florida).

With my required gear in hand I headed south to the promised land. It wasn't the one I pictured . . . the one flowing with milk and honey (a.k.a. the sliding glass door that opened onto the beach, cute guys, and decent food). This promised land left a whole lot to be desired. There were room checks, lights-out, and a window (where the sliding glass door was supposed to be) that I couldn't open without getting demerits.

Now, this educational institution did not seem the natural choice for someone like me. I was a kid who didn't grow up with many rules, because my behavior didn't warrant much policing (I know you're surprised). I was raised to be independent, honest, and most of all myself, which essentially translated to orneriness. I have fun and I enjoy life, which makes some people a little uncomfortable. (I made *all* the deans *really* nervous!)

Now, by most standards, I was a good kid who had managed to avoid the deep pitfalls of major trouble growing up. I didn't smoke, drink, or sleep around (which came in handy when I had to sign my tobacco-and-alcohol-free statement). Well, when I went to college, the standards regarding "trouble" changed. I was deemed an outright rebel without a cause (unbeknownst to them, I had a cause . . . it was the clue I was missing!). Most of my college peers had been a part of the parochial education system their entire lives, so they knew the drill and were used to the rules and regulations. On the other hand, this mangy product of the public school system was doing it backwards. I had seemingly walked from freedom into the law and was now caught in quicksand with no escape (we had big gates—supposedly to keep people out, not in).

While my schoolmates were studying for Bible class and English literature, I was busy greasing doorknobs, having ice fights, and creating elaborate "powder bombs." This was college, for crying out loud. Do I love Jesus? You bet, but study constantly? What—are you kidding me? My brand-new King James Version of the Bible had a verse right there in 1 Corinthians 9:1: "Am I not free?" There was more to life than just studying and going to church, and I only had seventeen and a half hours of "legal" awake time per day to discover it all.

Having been educated on the "outside world," I was the one who had the knowledge to carry out the masterful schemes, the likes of which most of them had never imagined. Therefore, I was automatically "the wild one." Fortunately (or unfortunately, depending on how you look at it), living up to my "reputation" was not difficult there. I earned demerits for such things as "popping my straw in the Varsity Commons" during our required dinners and more simple rebellious things like not making my bed for our daily inspection . . . however, usually only if I was still in it. (I'm not sure I count that as rebellion—laziness, maybe.)

It was a protected environment (apart from students like me, that is) in which people from all over the world sent their kids to essentially be parented by the college. We had a dress code and a hair code, strict rules governing dating, and required church attendance. Going to a movie could get you expelled, and as for tobacco and alcohol . . . well, if you admitted on your honesty statement that you had partaken in the past so many months, you got a nice little note to go meet with the deans about it. We didn't dance, gamble, swear, study past lights-out, ride mixed elevators, or have the opposite sex escort us back to the dorm after the sun had set, and if anyone did, the deans had eyes everywhere and knew about it every time.

As for romantic inclinations, the dean, floor leaders, prayer group leaders, and school administrators didn't have to worry about me. I was still trying to excise myself from the "farmer" boyfriend I dated all through high school. It was a relationship mostly of convenience and comfort that had no long-term potential. I was on the prowl for a husband, and I knew I'd find him there at college; otherwise, the statistics dictated that I would never find anyone!

Pity Dates 101

Since nothing else was normal at my educational institution, why would dating be any different? Regular "dating" pretty much consisted of going to church together. "Special occasion" dates were available when we had a vespers service or a fine arts concert or an operetta where we got all "black tie" fancied up for the evening. Usually we just moaned about it because it was required attendance, and we would, of course, have rather been studying (ha!).

We had our own Christian versions of sororities or fraternities called collegians, which left out all the partying, hazing, and general mayhem. However, the big highlight of the semester was an event the collegians called a "dating outing." Basically, in the spring it kind of worked like the Sadie Hawkins dances of junior high school where the girls ask the guys, and then in the fall, the natural order where the guys would request the girls' accompaniment.

My freshman year, I was brave. I asked a really cute guy I was interested in. We had a great time, and I got the proverbial pity date on Sunday. Now, I call them pity dates because I think the guy feels it's obligatory after a girl has taken him out on a dating outing. We pretty much deemed it "bad form" to go to church with a different girl the day after such an event where a girl had paid big bucks (anything over five dollars in college falls under the heading "big bucks," right?) to touch a guy's hand for a two-minute game. A mere two weeks later, the guy I took started dating a girl and was engaged by the next semester. Okey dokey! No problems here. We had fun, and I certainly didn't have any kind of dibs on him. End of the year, with one whopping pity date under my belt, I praised the Lord for His provision to get me a date but asked that He might try to arrange a few more next year.

My sophomore year, running off a steady diet of attending church with my roommates, I again braved my fear of rejection and asked my suitemate's brother. His sister was a great friend and I kind of had a little crush on him, so it seemed like a good idea at the time. He was a super sweet guy. Saturday we had witty conversation, enjoyable company, and even a couple hand-holding games, and I left feeling pretty good about the day. I again was awarded my Sunday pity date. As if the memo had been sent to him, two weeks later he, too, started dating the woman he ended up marrying. Well, after round two of the two-week bug, I was starting to get a bit of a complex. It was almost as if they were like, "Wow . . . I don't want to get stuck with her! I better find something else and quick!" Please note, the following two years repeated the scenarios with new guys, names left out to protect the guilty, stupid, or otherwise. Need I note that they both had similar quick-mating results? Hanging the bargain-basement price tag on my self-worth, I endured my four years of college with the four corresponding pity dates in the spring. I never did get asked in the fall. (Awwww.)

A Dating Drought

Some of us just do not date, period. We have no understanding of why we don't, we just know we don't. We are nice people, who regularly bathe and have what we consider to be the same average odds of finding someone special, especially when we see the guy we like with his pick of the week. *What is he thinking? What about me?* Which quickly develops into, *What about me is such a huge turnoff that I can't land a Friday night out?* In that case (which is generally my case), I don't really have any sound advice. The only thing I can say is that when I'm more active socially, I have more dating outings. Eventually, some guy is going to wake up and realize what a great catch we truly are, but the bottom line is that we have to be somewhere they can realize this.

Those who would like to date, but don't, often comment that dating is pretty much overrated. (Kind of along the same line of married people's telling us that sex is no big deal. It's no big deal because they are having it.) Take it from one who has dated in abundance and also endured fasts, dating is a big deal, and it isn't overrated. (Even though my definition of *dating* is two people pretending to be something they are not in order to trick or confuse the other party into buying the goods before they discover the truth.) It doesn't take a rocket scientist to discover that false realities and pretensions dictate most dating relationships in that most people try to impress the other person. (Review Chapter 4 if you have to!) However, dating is often some kind of social-acceptance thing. One of the main reasons people date is so they can finally tell someone, "I have a date!" They don't even care if it's awful. For some reason we earn brownie points for just being worthy of an outing.

That's not technically how you are supposed to handle dating, but then again who makes the rules, anyway? Married people? It's not like I'm going to marry the guy after one date, right? So what happens if you have never even had a date? Never fear! Many would argue that remaining a non-dating member of society is the smartest decision you could make! Personally, when I am not all worried about what someone thinks of me or what I will wear, I am a lot happier (and I have a lot more money because I'm not out buying new clothes all the time!). Going out these days is more about not being alone than it is about desire. There are plenty of real-life pity dates out there, but for now, I'd rather skip quantity and choose quality.

A perfect example would be the car salesman I went out with. The date transpired because he said he would take me out if I bought the vehicle since I would be his first sale. (Truth be told, I bought the car in part just to get the date!) I have had some just lovely blind date setups, which I will lump into the pity (or pitiful) date category. (Side note: You really find out what your friends think of you by who they set you up with. I am never sure if I am supposed to be grateful for their effort or appalled at their choice of potential mates for me. Mostly, I am just appalled, but I am still learning how to keep it to myself.)

It seems, at least in my life, good relationships with men come along about as often as the Publisher's Clearing House van. There are cycles, kind of like feast or famine, with me and dating. I have gone out with seven different guys at once, and I have had the "non-self-imposed" dating fast, which lasted three years. (I'm apparently gearing up to break the record right now.) The one thing I can identify is that in the past, my "outings" have been directly correlated to my opinion of myself (However, these days

I really think it's because I'm never in the state where I reside). When I am feeling fine, having good hair days, and find myself on top of the world, I'm beating them off the doorstep! When I'm having a "chubby period," and my hair is being squirrelly, and I feel like a burden on society, I am a drain sucking the life out of others . . . and I am alone. My theory holds water; I can mark it on a chart. If you aren't dating or haven't ever had a date, ask yourself these questions:

1. How is my relationship with Christ?
2. Do I spend time in fellowship and worship with my Creator?
3. Does my countenance show that I am His?
4. Do I love myself, and am I really open to being loved?
5. How do I portray myself to others? Do I act like I'm a worthless pest or show that I am a smart, funny, valuable person?
6. Do I ever leave my comfort zone? (i.e., do you go out to where other people are functioning healthily, which I can assure you is not in your living room with your pet.)
7. What can I do to change my perspective?
8. Am I currently the right one for someone else, or do I still have work to do?
9. Am I approachable?
10. Am I even willing and able to pour my life into someone else?

These questions are just a few to get you moving in the right direction. You really have to find out who you are and what will work for you. If you don't have a date to kiss good-bye, then you might need to find out what you are doing to drive the men off. Keep in mind, it also might be that the Lord is trying to keep you free from distraction so He can teach you some things first. If you are spending time with the Lord, you'll find your answer. Trust me, when we don't take time to be with and worship Him, it shows. We are cranky and irritable. Anything that has breath can praise the Lord (Ps. 150:6), but when we worship Him, something different transpires! Mountains are moved, people are healed, and our problems fade away.

There are days when I think I would make a fantastic girl-friend or wife, but there are also days when I really have to ground myself and get back to who I'm supposed to be. I'm busy being the right one. For who? Christ. I'm busy about His work, serving my peers and pouring my life into His ministers, ministry, and my friends, which is where I have been called. I'm not worried, because the Lord has called me to serve Him. If He chooses to provide a mate, then awesome. If not, I have work to do! So what if I don't have a date to kiss good-bye? I have a worship session scheduled!

⁓

I don't know if I can say I feel your pain or not, girl. I think I've broken the record on the man-fast and not-dating categories. With the exception of a brief fling several years ago, I can't even recall the last time I dated. That's not to say I haven't been out to dinner with a man or gone to an occasional movie over the years, but they were all my buddies or big brothers, nothing of the romantic persuasion. Early on I took it quite personally. I would gaze into the mirror hard and long, looking for warts I might have missed, but upon finding none decided that perhaps I was in a season God had not informed me about. As time went on, I actually failed to notice my dating drought. I was busy, productive, and had a host of nutty male friends who were attentive and kept me entertained; therefore, I ceased to keep track of how many days, months, and years rolled by with no physical romance in my life.

Laying the Foundation

I say *physical* romance because I was having a great time with the Lord all by myself. I was really settling into being spoiled by Him. Each day became a new adventure to see what lovely little surprise He would cook up for me. Chance encounters, new opportunities, little interesting experiences that filled my days with too much stuff to notice any empty spaces.

Once I stopped to ask, "Is this abnormal? Shouldn't a woman be stressed out about not having a man in her life?" To which He answered, "I don't want you to think about or ask Me about a man for a year. I want your full attention this entire year because I am laying a foundation for the rest of your life." On that note I said all right, and we were off and running. It was the year my new career as an author and speaker began. It was packed with so much activity I had little time to think of anything except the tasks at hand. At the end of the year I stopped and said, "Lord, I think I need another year to myself. I simply have too much to do right now to have my attention divided!" I couldn't believe I was saying it, but I really meant it! It's amazing what discovering your purpose and getting busy in it will do. It quickly rearranges your priorities. Since that time I have not looked back. I have come to the conclusion that when it's time, all the pieces will fall into place with no struggle involved, and I will find myself in a new season with some man saying, "Where are you going, and when will you be back?" In the meantime, I'm taking advantage of the time I have to get as much done as possible so that I will be able to slow down without feeling guilty about it.

The Manager's Choice

I've mentioned this before in my book *What to Do Until Love Finds You,* but I think it is appropriate to reiterate this here. While you are so busy trying to just throw your heart in the air and pray that someone catches it, consider the value of what you are flinging to high heaven. In God's eyes you are so very precious. Your price is far above rubies (Prov. 31:10), which were extremely expensive in the time that verse was written because they were rare. You are rare and unique; there is no one on the face of the earth like you. You are what I call one of the manager's choice jewels. Discerning jewelry shoppers know that there are different levels of jewelry. There's junk or costume jewelry—it's not real. It sits on the counter at any store with easy access to passersby. They can stop, touch it, try it on, and put it back if they don't like what it adds to them. Next!

Then there's fine jewelry. It is displayed under glass. You have to ask for permission to get a closer look. It's real. The price can range from reasonable to expensive. It is available to be tried on for the asking. It can be touched, held up, fitted, examined, and refused if the interested buyer decides they don't want to pay the price. Obviously they liked it, since they asked to take a closer look. Of course, after seeing it up close and personal they might discover it wasn't what they wanted after all. Some may like what they see; in that case, the decision boils down to if they still want it after they discover the cost, which is not readily known before taking it out of the case. Sometimes fine jewelry goes on sale. Sometimes the buyer will simply wait for the cost to go down before making a decision to purchase it. Hmm . . . Do you see where I'm going? Next!

I think this is where we come in. The manager's choice jewels are not even on the floor! They are in the back in a safe. He has to go back and get them to show to the more serious, discerning shopper. This shopper usually knows what he is looking for and asks specific questions. "Do you have a diamond of between two and three carats, clear with no inclusions?" Well! That's going to be expensive! That's when the manager goes to his safe and comes back with a little black velvet box that holds stars from the sky. He won't touch them with his fingers lest the oils affect its glow. He selects one with his special tool and secures it before holding it to the light for the admirer to behold its beauty. He hands him a jeweler's glass so that he can see for himself the quality of the stone. The beauty of its facets, the fire within it, the perfection. Sometimes there might be the slightest flaw, but it doesn't take away from the beauty. Only a discerning eye can truly appreciate this stone and know its worth. You are that stone. Until the right man comes along who is willing to pay the cost for you, the manager (God) is going to keep you in His safe, away from curious eyes and casual shoppers. Remember only the right setting (or man) can do full justice to a fine diamond.

Don't take it personally if there is no long line at your door; just remember that you are being kept by the Almighty. "He [or she] that dwelleth in the secret place of the Most High shall abide under the shadow of the Almighty" (Ps. 91:1 KJV). How sweet is that? What do you do in the meantime? Worship Him; practice being intimate with the Lover of your soul. Your capacity to love the man He puts before you will parallel your ability to love the Man who is already in your life—Christ Jesus. Draw close and let Him teach you how to love.

But could Mr. Right have gotten away and I didn't know it, Michelle? I doubt it. No one can snatch what God has for you.

If you passed it by, God is able to bring you full circle back to that place again. He does it with every other lesson we try to skip. No, I dare to say that you are exactly where you should be right now. Be patient, and he will come not a moment too soon or a second too late.

13 Every Date Is a Potential Mate

"For I know the plans I have for you," declares the LORD, "plans to prosper you and not to harm you, plans to give you hope and a future."

—JEREMIAH 29:11 NIV

If I were Catholic, at this point I would no doubt be "Sister Holly," tooling around the nunnery. My friends can't see it . . . me with my skirt tucked between my legs and my habit pushed back behind my ears, being sporty Sister Holly; for some reason it just doesn't fly with them. I'm agreeable to it only because I know I'd be the good-humored one—you know, the "flying nun" character. I've been down the road of absolutely horrid dates and some days find that I am so done with the whole dating arena that I'm almost willing to sign up . . . almost. (That whole celibacy-forever thing is a very long-term commitment, and I think I might still have a shot.)

While sometimes it's hard to understand just why, we do have to date to eventually mate. If you've developed your images of dating from a stringent Bible-believing home, you have most undoubtedly limited yourself to only chaperoned rendezvous until the age of twenty-one (at least that's how it was in college!). If not, dating probably falls somewhere between that and having no regulations other than the mere goal of seek and find. As a general rule, we have to date or essentially spend time getting to know someone (in some cases many someones) until we find the perfect fit for us.

When you go to the car dealership, paying the sticker price will allow you to own that car. However, that is not the final cost of the vehicle. When contemplating your purchase, you have to consider what that vehicle will cost you in gas, insurance, and maintenance. There is a big difference in being able to afford the initial price of something versus the final cost of something.

In dating, you need to evaluate that price and the cost. Dating (which should not be confused with a primarily physical relationship) should simply be a means for us to obtain the knowledge we need to make an informed decision about choosing a mate. If you eventually desire to tie the knot, there is a certain protocol that necessitates spending time with someone in order to enter into a marriage relationship. I don't suppose it's necessarily mandatory, but it is certainly advisable. (Chapter 15, "Check for Worms Before You Take a Bite of the Apple," will help clear that up for you!)

When you go out with someone, you are able to collect information on the cost of this relationship. Does this person fill you, or does he emotionally bankrupt you? Does he enhance your relationship with the Lord, or is he simply distracting you from spending time with Him? Based on the facts and the evaluations you make, you can choose to move forward for more intense and personal "data collection" (ladies, to clarify, this does not mean we get his boxer size for gifts or what kind of cologne he wears so we can spray our bears!), head into a committed (courting-type) relationship, or break off the relationship entirely.

Dating, for better or for worse, is a large part of life for most singles. Yes, even if you fall into the "lack thereof" category where I tend to camp. In fact, it is one of the essential aspects of single life (contented or discontented) if we are truthful. Good days and bad days rise and fall on whether we even have a date (or if we have something to wear that makes us look stunning if we do have one). Whether we are actively out on the town or fasting from it all, it's an innate part of our thought processes. Through the years, people have experimented with every kind of dating relationship arrangement possible.

COURTING VS. DATING

Dating, as we know it today, has largely evolved over the past hundred or so years. As the evolution of dating morally continues to nosedive, surely there has to be a better answer. Let me first address the fact that there has been a lot of controversy over the terminology of the word *date* in the Christian scene. Somewhere the memo got passed around that you are not a godly person unless you plan on courting your future mate. Everyone has a personal system for developing relationships. If your personality finds it difficult to commit to a courting relationship without the gathering-data phase, then you're probably in the larger of the two camps. Keep in mind, you need to go about developing the relationships in your life in a way that works for you. Pressure for you to fit your life into the set pattern of courting when you don't understand it or enjoy it will only cause frustration. There are certainly godly ways to date, and there are surely ungodly ways to court. Do what is right for you . . . but do it according to what the Lord would have you do!

I encourage you to pray about how God would have you follow through with relationship developing. No matter what you call it, the principles found here are applicable wherever you are in your Christian walk and to whatever means you choose to use. I use the term "dating" simply because it is a more generalized term that everyone easily recognizes. Some may not understand the concept of courting (if you want more information on it, I suggest you pick up *I Kissed Dating Goodbye* or *Boy Meets Girl* by Joshua Harris). Whether you date, court, dream of dating or courting, or invent pretend husbands, this chapter is foundational.

Female Seeking Male

I'm confident, as a seasoned single, that most of us are pretty tired of books and seminars with "rules" that merely throw out lame suggestions on finding a man. It seems to me that the "goods" never quite seem to come in. As a result of friendly demands, I have been "done in" by several well-meaning pals who have sent me to some of those meat-market seminars or who have bought me outrageous numbers of books on dating as if I were stupid and did it wrong. (Of course since my married friends' verbal advice is so bad, I guess I actually appreciate the books, since two of them were Michelle's!)

There are also the friends who have seemingly dedicated their lives to finding us mates. You know the ones. They are the brave few who are devoted, no matter the price, to finding us *the one*. It generally starts with their setting us up with some distant relative four times removed. My well-meaning friends generally provide minimal details, such as that the candidate is of the opposite sex and walks upright. To compensate for the bad blind dates, they take out newspaper ads in the personals for us, sign us up for dating services, and scan the horizon for any other potential companions. (One friend even offered to take me on an all-expense-paid trip to Alaska for a week to do some serious man-hunting. I passed but appreciated the offer anyway.)

Of course, the problem with these setups is that they leave us to deal with the crazies they drag up. Generally they are co-dependent dysfunctional oddities who barely have a pulse or evidence of brain activity. But really, it's the effort that counts, right? (Eye roll—unfortunately, the efforts of our friends are where we base our hope, so we can't cut them off completely!) All that said, we're tired of following the unspoken plan, sacrificing our self-esteem and ideals, only to continue to pitch our tent in the camp of Soloville.

FUNNELING THE RISKS

For the most part, though, I consider myself to be a risk-taking person. Everything I do gets strained through the net of "What is the worst-possible-case scenario?" For instance, I moved to Nashville, Tennessee, several years ago. I didn't have a job, I didn't know anyone, and I didn't have too terribly much to call my own. I knew the Lord was calling me to move, but I fought tooth and nail with Him on it, confident that I was just reading into His will for me. Once I got to the place I was sure He wanted me to be, I conceded to His plan. The human side of me was still whispering, *What if it doesn't work out? What if I hate it? What if I fail?* My logical side countered, *What is the worst-possible-case scenario? I fail . . . I move home and live with my parents.* If that happens, will it affect my relationship with Christ? *Nope.* Will it change my testimony? *Shouldn't.* Will I live through it? *More than likely.* So what if I fail . . . I'll still have Christ, I highly doubt that I will starve to death, and I will have at least tried. I've discovered that "What if I don't fail?" is a much better tree to nest in! As God would have it, my successes have been considerably greater than my failures. I regularly launch out into the unknown and am usually much better for it. All that to say: Brave the crazy dates, you might just end up with Mr. Right.

THIS MIGHT BE THE ONE

I must point out that while every date could potentially be a mate, we don't necessarily date for the exclusive privilege of mating. Huh? We should enter dating similarly to how we shop. Pick it up, check it out by inspecting the goods, determine the value, ask yourself if you really need it, and finally, evaluate to see if it's worth the cost. Michelle uses a great illustration on the price of something versus the cost of owning something.

Men (I am sure) hate the mentality that every date could actually be a potential mate. The last thing most of them are considering on the first date is marriage. But it boils down to this: If you don't like what you see on the first couple of dates, then it might be best to sever that dating connection. It is advisable, of course, to remain friends, but I do not suggest comfort dating, or essentially finding someone (anyone) to date, or consistently "hanging out" just for the sake of not being alone. Having male friends is one thing, but having male friends you are interested in is another. Set up realistic boundaries (even if just in your mind) in case a male friend leads to the role of boyfriend!

I realize that it is common practice to have a "not so special someone" to call your very own. Just someone out there floating around who sort of cares for you, at least in a pinch. However, sexual relationships and compromising situations are oftentimes born out of boredom more than desire. In our effort to fulfill our passions and "dreams," we often conform to the world and use its yardstick as the dictating standard. "Everyone is

doing it" becomes our excuse, and soon we are falling into pitfalls we actually laid for ourselves. Remember the flee theory in
Chapter 9?

TEMPORARY RAIN TO EASE THE DROUGHT

I mentioned my date with the car salesman a chapter back. Let
me fill you in on the actual date! He was a great guy who was
very sweet and surprisingly romantic. When I was in the process
of buying my vehicle from him, I had asked about which transmission I would need, due to the fact that I was getting that
vehicle essentially so that I could pull a speedboat to the lake. I
bought the "souped-up" vehicle in light of his recommendation
and never had a problem towing my boat to the lake (well, save
the time a car hit me, but that wasn't a transmission issue). Upon
the fulfillment of my purchase, he dutifully lived up to his end
of the bargain by taking me out.

Of course, I would have settled for McDonald's just to be out
with a man (especially one who was buying). Anything to break
the seemingly endless drought! However, he was very in tune to
me as a person. He remembered from the car transaction that I
enjoyed boating, so he actually took me to a floating restaurant
at one of the marinas here in town. I was impressed! Talk about
a dreamboat (no pun intended)!

It was a fantastic night, and I was most definitely interested!
On our second "date," he took me downtown for a fun night out
where we ate a romantic dinner and walked around the main
drag in Nashville. He was 100 percent sweet, cute, charming,
romantic, and affectionate. When the offer for date number three
rolled around, I was torn. Quite frankly, I liked him, but he wasn't
the best choice for me, and I knew it. Unfortunately, everything
boiled down to the fact that he really was not pursuing an active

relationship with Christ and was certainly nowhere near the spiritual leader I am looking for to lead my heart. Ugh, so now what?

As much as I enjoyed being around him in all the other facets, I severed the dating ties (citing the reason in hopes he'd step up to the call—unfortunately, he didn't), and we both moved on. We're still friends and I see him from time to time . . . and wow, I loved being with him, but I know that ultimately it was the right decision for me. I'm really very good at evangelism dating.

So, in summary, what I've come to embrace is that every date, every gaze, every discussion, every interaction with someone is an opportunity for you to more vividly recognize and determine what you really want. I think discovery is important (with firm boundaries, however, for those of you whose mind just wandered). The key is to stay focused on your desires, be true to the Lord, follow your heart, and be bound by your values. You don't have to beat down doors or fight someone for the honor of having them in your life. It should be an obvious and natural progression.

I've had a lot of dates but not so many potential mates. However, I'm not willing to throw in the towel just yet . . . because I know what I'm looking for, and I know that he's out there somewhere, looking for me!

ℯ〜

Let me don the habit here and be Mother Superior (after all, it is age before beauty). There is a fine line here that must be drawn. Yes, every date is a potential mate; however, that should not be your first thought when meeting someone. Approach every date as a potential friend, someone God directed into your life so you can leave a lasting deposit of His Spirit within him. Whether he is saved or unsaved, you, as a woman, have the incredible power to transform that man into a vessel of honor by your quiet influence. By the way you live your life before him.

AT FACE VALUE

Early on in my Christian walk I met many unsaved men I was interested in. I allowed my interest in them to distract me from the true purpose for their being in my life—to introduce them to Christ. Not by witnessing to them every time I saw them, but by being a godly friend. Jesus walked with many who were considered heathen; He took the time to talk and interact with them, to build relationships with them. It was through relationship they were converted. Now hold up here! When I say "relationship," I am not speaking of *romantic* relationship, I am talking about walking with a person through the everyday paces of life as a friend, one they come to trust to offer input into their lives when they ask for it. Remember, uninvited counsel is seldom received.

I think we too often cut off all access because a man is not saved, and thereby ruin the opportunity to win him to Christ. Remember one of the first commands we are given is to be fruitful and multiply. This addresses more than the natural act of procreation—God wants us to be fruitful by multiplying the kingdom of God. It takes relationships in order to make this occur. Jesus was a relationship kind of guy. He wasn't interested in marrying the women He met, yet He took the time to walk with them, to reveal the kingdom of God and its truths to them. It's as if we decide that a man can't be anything to us at all if he can't be exactly what we pictured him as. Jesus did not discount people that way. How about just dealing with that person at face value? No, he is not saved. No, he does not qualify as mate material for me at this time; however, he's a good man who needs to know Jesus. I know Jesus. Perhaps I can make the introduction once I have gained his trust. Hmm, we don't like to go there. Why? Because of the fear of falling.

That's right. You don't want to do the work it takes to stand on your square. You don't want to set the boundaries and guard your heart while learning how to be a true friend to someone who actually needs you. Women need to learn how to be friends with men. It is actually great practice for marriage because you should marry your best friend. You need to *like* your husband as well as love and be in love with him. How can you be friends with your husband if you never learn to be friends with men?

I, too, was guilty of this for quite some time. I did not know how to have platonic relationships with men. Every man I met had to fit into the romantic mold or they just didn't fit into my life at all. I am happy to say that today I have a lot of male friends, saved and unsaved, who are supportive and loving. None of them would ever consider having me compromise my faith, and those who are unsaved know the requirements if they desire to be involved with me on any other level than friendship. I've drawn clear lines, and no one is crossing them. I see those who are not believers slowly approaching the faith pool, no longer resisting the waters, because my friendship has caused Jesus to look inviting, rather than religious and judgmental.

Missionary dating? I do not recommend it by any means. We are all too vulnerable when longing for love, and let's face it, it's just as easy to fall in love with an unsaved man as a saved man. Sad but true, sometimes those uncircumcised Philistines are more interesting than those who belong to the house of faith. However, if Jesus truly is a part of your life, there is only so far you can go with them. There is a major part of yourself that you will never be able to share and have them comprehend, and it will become a hindrance to true intimacy with them.

THE WOMAN AT THE WELL

I will add that I believe Jesus makes us attractive for a reason. I think of the Samaritan woman at the well, in John chapter 4, who definitely knew how to get a man, whether she kept him or not. When she finished speaking with Jesus and got a revelation of who He was, the story goes that she went back to town to *the men*. What men? The men she had been associating with, had slept with, who knew her reputation and visited her house. She told them all about her experience of meeting Jesus, and they all followed her to see what she was talking about, met Jesus, and believed on Him, too. They then told her, "Now we believe, not because of what you told us but because we have seen for ourselves." She was not a contingency to their faith; they grabbed their newfound faith and ran with it. What are you showing the men in your life? Are you showing them just what you want or need from them, or are you showing them Jesus?

Can you lead that man to the well and then release him to grow in the things of God without getting your heart involved? If you do, you will get to see how serious he is. If you are the catalyst for his salvation experience, it is crucial that he have the attitude of those men from Samaria: *Now I believe, but I will take it from here.* Let him find brothers to walk with to mentor him in his faith, continue to be his friend, and see what happens. Perhaps he could be the one for you, perhaps not. Don't get hung up on the span of years that a man knows the Lord. Time has nothing to do with it; commitment and passion do. I have seen many a man take off in the things of the Lord, become a sold-out leader, and surpass men who have been in the church all their lives. Again this can have a lot to do with your influence. Walk with open hands. There are many in my life who were saved and married other women. I fulfilled my purpose and released them. I believe they are better men today because of my influence.

I hear this phrase a lot: "I want a man who can lead me in the things of the Lord." Yet the reality is, that role will go back and forth in a marriage with the seasons of our lives. Sometimes up, sometimes down—our faith fluctuates. Though the man is supposed to be the spiritual leader, we all are stronger in different points of our faith. Here is where a wife can build up her husband and inspire him to new heights in various aspects of his beliefs and convictions. Women tend to be more sensitive spiritually overall, but that doesn't mean that men are not strong in their faith, they are just geared more to the bottom line because of their makeup. At times the woman may seem to hear more from God than her husband does, at other times the husband will hear more. This is what a yoke is all about. The preference is that they carry equal weight, but sometimes that is not the case. Life happens to all of us, and the spiritual load will be shared by both. Sometimes one will have to carry what the other is unable to bear at the time. That is why two are better than one—they help each other as they rise and fall. The only man who will constantly be your spiritual leader is your pastor, and even he is subject to fall in the midst of his humanity.

GETTING REAL

Women must get rid of unrealistic expectations. It is realistic to want a man who knows and loves God. A man who doesn't want to break God's heart, because then he won't break yours.

You want a man who hears from God and obeys. You want a man who can get a prayer through. A man who knows he has a purpose and is actively pursuing it. If he doesn't know it, he is open to being inspired to locate it. The end.

A soul mate? Or spirit mate? What many do not realize is that God is your soul mate. You are an extension of His Spirit. He breathed the breath of life into you that made you a living soul. That is the craving you feel—to be joined back to Him in an eternal kiss that will complete you. No man has that power. Even when you get married, that craving will remain until you establish the grounds for intimacy and balance your heart between God and man. As you focus on filling the God-shaped hole in your heart with God Himself, you will be able to be freer in your interactions with men in your life because you won't be looking to them to fill spaces in you they are not supposed to fill. The results? A happier, healthier you. One who is able to rejoice in each and every day and every opportunity for new and rich friendships. The ability to be clear about the purpose for each one. Seizing every opportunity to make an impact for the kingdom simply by being the woman you are, and loving every minute of it.

14 The Backup Plan

I will fear no evil; for You are with me.

—PSALM 23:4 NKJV

If there is a chapter in this book that is most frequently "lived out" on TV, it's this one. It seems every program on the picture tube or big screen promotes the backup-plan theory. A Plan B substitute for the best and real thing. Movies like *As Good As It Gets* and *The Next Best Thing* and a slew of others promote settling for second best.

I'm not endorsing any program here, but have you seen the *Friends* (I know you watch it) episode where Matthew Perry's character, Chandler Bing, realizes his likeness to Mr. Heckles, an obnoxious neighbor who passed away leaving his possessions to the yuppies? Bing, realizing his life parallels the miserable old man's, calls his former girlfriend Janice, in a bit of a panic. Janice is annoying, loud, whiney, and certainly not the best option for

Chandler. However, in desperation, he rationalizes to the friends that she is his last chance to be with anyone. She is better than the option of being alone.

Ever done that? Gone back to an old flame out of fear of being alone only to realize that the relationship was horrible then, and it's horrible now? Still it's something, it's someone, and it might be better than being alone, right? Or are you a proponent of the explicit backup plan? You know the plan, where there's a person who isn't "in love with you" or "good enough" to marry right now . . . but "in case we make it to the ripe old age of forty and haven't struck gold, let's you and I hook up, okay?"

That's not the best plan, and I don't know how many people in real life marry their backup just to have companionship or some semblance of a family, but I assume that is not how God anticipated the whole process. I want someone who is in love with me and targeted on God!

Since my status in life is single right now, I choose not to hang out just waiting for something that may never happen. Here I am, Lord. I'm ready to go; send me! As I have traveled extensively with artists, some common themes play themselves out over and over again. Churches do not know what to do with the singles, yet they are quickly becoming the majority. Many of us are made to feel like second-class citizens as functions for youth, college, and married couples are announced in the church bulletin weekly, and countless seminars are offered to teach married couples how to get along with one another. Yet not enough people address how singles can be victorious alone. It sometimes seems that nobody is out there validating our emotions and struggles. Doesn't anyone "get" it?

After you've outgrown your College and Careers class, which is programmed for eighteen- to twenty-three-year-olds, you are pretty much on your own. Rarely does anyone stress the importance of identifying a single person's life purpose or helping to equip them with the tools to become modern-day Pauls in the twenty-first century. There are seminars for married people on how to be better mates and more effective parents, and other conferences on subjects related to them or their families. All the while, singles sit on the sidelines with little or no programming designed for us. There certainly isn't any hand-holding or coddling involved! Often, we attend a Sunday school class with people twice our age and generally only Christ in common, or we teach a class for other people's kids and cringe when our name is called preceded by a "Mrs." we haven't earned. Churches aren't going to change their focus to include us overnight, and it's not actually their job to spoon-feed us anyway. It's up to us to find our purpose!

All I'm stressing is the importance of identifying your life purpose. It's up to you to equip yourself with the tools to become like the apostle Paul in the twenty-first century. You and I have the same Bible with the same information. The difference is how we internalize the gospel and how we apply it to our lives.

STRAIGHT AS AN ARROW

I was visiting a church where the youth pastor was explaining how we were arrows. I couldn't help but make the application to my life. Isaiah says: "He made my mouth like a sharpened sword, in the shadow of his hand he hid me; he made me into a polished arrow and concealed me in his quiver" (Isa. 49:2 NIV).

In light of the fact that He apparently makes us into polished arrows, there are some things we need to understand about the creation of arrows in order to grasp the importance. Unbeknownst to me, there is a fine art to the creation of an arrow. There is little margin for error as the arrow is created for one specific purpose—

to be shot toward a target or goal. Most important, there is the selection of the entire basis of the arrow—the wood, which becomes the shaft, the foundation of the arrow.

SELECTION OF THE WOOD

Now, there isn't a magic arrow tree, you know. So the selection of the type of wood is very important. An arrow needs to be constructed from heavy, strong timber so it can withstand the strain of being fired from a hundred-pound-plus bow (that is the force) and also be able to impact an animal or a steel plate without shattering. Not just any tree will do. Cedar, pine, and fir are the most common wood types because of their strength. God selects us in the same way. "You did not choose me, but I chose you and appointed you to go and bear fruit—fruit that will last" (John 15:16 NIV). Have you ever thought to consider that the Lord has chosen you because you have an innate strength He would like to use for a specific purpose? One He gave and anointed you for?

PAINS OF PRUNING

The next natural step involves the pruning of the branches. Ever seen an arrow flying through the sky with leaves still attached? If you have, it didn't go far! The extra weight and sprigs must be removed, or they will disrupt the air flow and agility of the arrow, causing it not to be as efficient. Similarly, God works in our life to remove those things that hinder our service for Him. "I am the true vine, and my Father is the gardener. He cuts off every branch in me that bears no fruit, while every branch that does bear fruit he prunes so that it will be even more fruitful" (John 15:1–2 NIV). God makes sure that He removes things from our life that will impede our flight. On the other hand, He sometimes adds to our life people and circumstances that we might not even enjoy for the sole purpose of drawing us to Himself so He can change us.

> And not only that, but we also glory in tribulations, knowing that tribulation produces perseverance; and perseverance, character; and character, hope. Now hope does not disappoint, because the love of God has been poured out in our hearts by the Holy Spirit who was given to us. (Rom. 5:3–5 NKJV)

STRAIGHTEN IT OUT

Now, wood doesn't just grow completely straight, and the shaft-making process does not turn out perfectly straight shafts on the first attempt. Wood can bend under stress or in differing humidity conditions or, ironically enough, just on its own—like us. All of that to say, arrow makers will straighten shafts several times during the arrow-making process. Then they continue to perform remedial straightening after the arrows have been shot.

Once a noticeable bend is sighted, the maker can try to preliminarily straighten it by rubbing another piece of wood against the outside of the bend. This actually compresses some of the cells in the wood and shortens that side so the shaft pulls back straight. Note how the maker uses the same material to encourage the wood to action. This is where our friends come into play. "As iron sharpens iron, so a man sharpens the countenance of his friend" (Prov. 27:17 NKJV). Our friends are similar to the arrow maker in this respect. The producer of the arrow doesn't want to press too hard (leaving dents in the shaft or even breaking it), but needs to be firm enough to compress some of the wood and encourage it back to the straight (and narrow) way. In the same fashion true friends pull you back to the Lord, not strong-arming, but firmly holding you to the truth. Proverbs says, "Faithful are the wounds of a friend" (27:6 NKJV). It may not feel good, but if you have the right people surrounding you in your life, they will hold you accountable and call you on things when you get a little too "curvy."

In order to further straighten a shaft, the best choice is to soak the wood in oil. This makes the wood much more pliable and willing to bend to the creator's wish without stressing (which weakens) the wood by force. If you try to bend a branch, it can break if pushed too far; but by softening the wood in oil, it becomes pliable, willing to bend. I find it interesting that the Lord used oil for similar purposes: "They drove out many demons and anointed many sick people with oil and healed them" (Mark 6:13 NIV). Notice the order: oil first and then the healing, which is analogous to the application of softening oil to the arrow before correction.

FEEL THE HEAT

Once the maker has allowed the arrow to soak in the oil for a predetermined period of time, he applies heat to get the "kinks" out. He places the arrow in the middle of the flame, using the heat to burn away all the impurities and to continue the straightening process. He cannot take his eyes off it, because it could become too hot and catch fire, completely destroying it. Instead, he continually twists the shaft, careful not to leave it in the hottest part of the flame too long. Sound vaguely familiar?

> In this you greatly rejoice, though now for a little while, if need be, you have been grieved by various trials, that the genuineness of your faith, being much more precious than

gold that perishes, though it is tested by fire, may be found to praise, honor, and glory at the revelation of Jesus Christ. (1 Peter 1:6–7 NKJV)

Read Jeremiah 17:7–8: "But blessed is the man who trusts in the LORD, whose confidence is in him. He will be like a tree planted by the water that sends out its roots by the stream. It does not fear when heat comes; its leaves are always green. It has no worries in a year of drought and never fails to bear fruit" (NIV). Feel the heat?

The final step in the shaft-creation process is to bind the refined arrow to two already tried-and-true, proven arrows. The two straight arrows finalize the straightening of the shaft under gentle guidance by example, drawing the shaft to their already perfected straightness. Isn't it just fitting that the commands of the Word line up with that?

Likewise, teach the older women to be reverent in the way they live, not to be slanderers or addicted to much wine, but to teach what is good. Then they can train the younger women to love their husbands and children, to be self-controlled and pure, to be busy at home, to be kind, and to be subject to their husbands, so that no one will malign the word of God. (Titus 2:3–5 NIV)

Similarly, encourage the young men to be self-controlled. In everything set them an example by doing what is good. In your teaching show integrity, seriousness and soundness of speech. (Titus 2:6–8 NIV)

MAKING A POINT

Once the shaft is as straight as the creator can make it, the arrow is completed by attaching the point and the flights (feathers that aid in airflow and guidance). It's finally time to shoot it. If you are truly the "arrow" God has been working on and refining for His service, then your cry should resemble this: "'Whom shall I send, and who will go for Us?' Then I said, 'Here am I! Send me'" (Isa. 6:8 NKJV).

What target are you shooting toward? One you have created or the one God has destined for you? Where do you find yourself in the refinement process? Are you seeking out the better thing or skipping steps and skirting the edge? Are you planning for compromise or leaning toward the best? An arrow flies alone, but someone has to shoot it. Where does your "flight" come from? When a master marksman is shooting toward a goal, he is trusting that the arrow he has chosen was created with care and accuracy. He's assuming that all the steps were in place to create the best arrow possible. The backup plan is a lot like just plucking a branch off a tree to use as an arrow and trying to hit the bull's-eye. You're never going to get the outcome you want without going through the right steps. Stay on target.

℮⁓

Well, Holly, I have to admit that I got carried away with the whole backup plan myself, and I've promised a couple of my male friends that if we're not married by a certain age I will marry them. (Just in case the first backup fell through I wanted to have a few more in reserve.) Unfortunately, I can't remember who I promised what first. I think I'm going to be in trouble! Perhaps they've also forgotten by now. To be perfectly honest, I think we've all lost count of what year we made this nutty promise anyhow.

Now girl, all that talk about straightening the arrow sounded painful! Sounded like my life early on. No wonder I said "Ouch!"

so much. I kept trying to live in God's "permissible" will, but I couldn't find a comfortable spot to save my soul. Then somebody pulled my coattail. "Uh . . . there's no such thing as His 'permissible' will, Michelle. He has only one will for your life, and it's good, acceptable, and perfect. There is no backup plan. Either do whatcha gotta do or get off the pot." Well, that was sobering. I thought there was a slide factor, and now I was being told there is only one way.

Boy, this Jesus was looking more strict by the minute. He was the only way to the Father and it was His way or the highway. The broad highway leads to destruction. This is where the struggle begins, when we realize that we must be politically incorrect to follow Christ. We must be narrow-minded. It is the narrow path that leads to life. That sounded horrible to me at first, but since I've started down the path I've found that there's a lot of room for a full, rich life on that road. I'm having the time of my life! I'm finding that the road doesn't feel as narrow as I thought it would. There is more liberty than I expected. Truly living in the truth sets us free from more than we initially think. Yes, there is abundant living on that road. Jesus promised that not only would we have life, but we would have it more abundantly; and if we keep our end of the bargain, it's ours for the living.

The Best Plan

The famous backup plan is only for those who don't trust God. They feel they have to help Him out just in case He doesn't deliver the goods. But that is futile thinking, because man is famous for letting you down. God can't let you down because He cannot lie. He's bound by His own Word to do what He said He would do in your life, on one condition—you hold up your end of the deal by making the right choices. You get to choose life or death, blessings or curses for your life every day. You obey His Word, and you get life and blessings. You disobey, and the door prize is death and curses. Death to the joy and peace you were looking for, sometimes more. I like the fact that God keeps it simple. We complicate it by trying to read between the lines to find the gray areas. Stop it! He means what He says, and says what He means.

I recently did a seminar on purity for teenagers. I had them submit questions for me to answer at the end of the workshop. I was shocked and appalled. "Can we touch this and it not be sin?" . . . "Can we do this or that?" . . . "Or how about . . . ?" Finally, I threw up my hands and threatened to put them all in straitjackets. "It's all sin!" I cried. "There's no two ways about it." Proverbs 6:27 says, "You cannot carry hot coals against your chest without burning your clothes" (NCV). Ezekiel 18:4 tells us, "The soul who sins shall die" (NKJV). There is no backup plan mentioned in Scripture. There are consequences for our disobedience, pure and simple, even if God forgives the sin. Why do we always try to stretch the envelope? To find the thin line that separates sin from righteousness? To skate across the grace of God and hope we don't hit a thin spot? We do the same thing with every area of our life; we want to skip the lessons and get to the prizes, and when they don't come soon enough—well, there's my stash of comforts I kept to the side just in case . . .

The bottom line of the backup plan is that we still love ourselves and what we want too much. No man can serve two masters; he will love one and despise the other (Luke 16:13). The other will be accused of being the culprit who keeps us from getting what we want. As we fight to hold on to the last vestiges of our own personal desires, we devise Plan B just in case God doesn't fulfill the desires of our hearts. But we really must get over ourselves. Face it, we will never be happy living in the land of compromised faith because it is not true kingdom living.

Here's the A plan: God's plan. That you experience what Adam and Eve experienced in Eden. The word *Eden* means "pleasure" or "delight." God wants us to know Him, love Him, and draw pleasure from our experiences with Him. It is then and only then that He can trust us and give us the other desires of our heart, knowing that we won't run off and forget about Him the minute we get what we've been longing for. Love Him enough to be completely obedient simply because you love Him, not because you've memorized a bunch of Bible verses. Compelled by love, you actually consider how God would feel about the things you choose to do and passionately choose not to do anything that would grieve His heart. Out of this loving obedience come righteousness (right relationship with Him), peace (when folks are getting along, ain't it nice and peaceful?), and joy in the Holy Ghost (a great sense of overall well-being that increases your joy in spite of any outward circumstances).

Jesus promised that the joy He gave was different from the world's offering of external happiness. The joy He gives comes from within and fills us with the assurance that God is on our side. And no matter what happens, we shall not be moved. We will stay on track until we reach our target—a joyful, fulfilled life. (How fabulous a plan is that? We're the only ones who can mess it up by having a mediocre mind-set. That sounds pretty dull to me, not the makings of an effective arrow by any stretch.)

Where are you in your attitude toward life? Are you going for the gold, or will you settle for a bronze coin? God won't force His plan on you, but He sure would be delighted to have you on the A team. Straight, strong, victorious, and cutting-edge. Piercing the darkness with your light, making an impact for the kingdom. Sounds like a plan to me. To settle for less than the best God has for you by refusing to wait only a little while longer is to rob yourself of the true happy ending of the story.

THE RIGHT ATTITUDE

Recently I was on a plane, and we had to land before the movie was over. It drove me crazy, because I couldn't find out what happened. If you get married just because you're tired of waiting, you will always live with the feeling of having settled for second-best every time something doesn't go the way you think it should in the relationship. But the worst part is, you will never get to know what God intended for you. It's like the arrow that hits the ground before it reaches its mark—anticlimactic. I can't stand to be left hanging when I'm near the end of a good plot, can you?

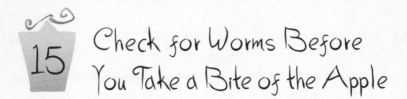

15 Check for Worms Before You Take a Bite of the Apple

The LORD does not see as man sees; for man looks at the outward appearance, but the LORD looks at the heart.

—1 SAMUEL 16:7 NKJV

I really can't recall the first time I heard the saying "Check for worms before you take a bite of the apple," but I have practiced the art religiously after several experiences gone bad. I check and double-check my fresh fruit snacks these days. Mostly out of paranoia, but perhaps partly out of sheer terror based on those past experiences. However, even after carefully inspecting my fresh snacks, on more than one occasion I have snagged an apple off our family tree in the backyard only to discover a couple of bites into it that something else had already been nibbling on the inside. At first glance it appeared "fine"; there was not always outside evidence that a critter (be it a bug or a worm) had taken over the interior. I plucked the fruit before its time, but allowing growth and maturity for the fruit in question would better

172

display the final product, and I've found the same to be true in relationships.

This simple lesson really boils down to this: If I had allowed the fruit to fully develop and ripen, it would have, more than likely, developed bruising and displayed "mushiness" at the point of entry, sparing me the many mini heart attacks and the spitting of apple flesh all over our yard during the summer. As far as that relates to the single life, in the same way, we will not always be able to tell if Mr. Wonderful is really everything he seems to be on the surface without the testing of time. Once you get past the skin, the insides might just be rotten!

Ironically enough (or moronically, if you will), I had my own real-life "rotten" apple relationship. I was involved with a guy I really thought was "the one." He was kind, considerate, generous, sweet, and, most of all, really liked me for me. I had not had many relationships like that in the past. Keep in mind, I was coming off the now infamous three-year drought, during which I had no dates at all. So when he treated me like a princess, well, duh! I was hooked! Other silly little things were adding up, too, and I was giddy with confidence that I was going to beat the self-imposed deadline of marriage by thirty. Never mind the fact that I was head over heels in love with the *idea* of being in love. Needless to say, I had a definite spring in my step.

About four months into the relationship, it dawned on me that I had not really noticed too many flaws. I came to the realization that perhaps I had been viewing him through the proverbial "rose-colored glasses." Recalling my commitment to the Lord to fully inquire of Him and be faithful to listen before I gave my heart away (notice that it was something I already had in place!), I earnestly started praying that the Lord would open my eyes and help me to see this man for who he really was. After all, we had begun to discuss marriage, kids, and building a home together! Once that prayer was uttered, my ideal man turned into an unbearable brute. The first red flag was that all of a sudden he was not as godly as he had seemed earlier. There was some newfound cussing, then the question changed from "What time is church?" to "Are we going to church?" Deep down, I knew I was in trouble, but maybe he was just having an "off" week, I rationalized. He certainly didn't do such things before my prayer!

I would later learn that he didn't really share my dedication to Christ, but simply wanted to make me happy. Not altogether a bad thing, as he was, at least temporarily, willing to fill that role as spiritual leader (even though he had no concept of what that meant). You get an A for effort, buddy, but your overall grade is sinking to failure fast! There were other indications that he might not be "the one": Around the same time, bathing, for some unknown reason, went out the window along with the brushing of the teeth. His gentleness was replaced with harshness and his understanding with obvious frustration. All of a sudden this guy, who I really thought was the one, was striking out every time he was at bat! I finally came to the place where I could not stand the thought of spending an evening with him, let alone my life! Eventually he was benched and traded to another team. However, if I had based my decision on the emotion we felt that first few months, I would have gotten into a disastrous relationship in the long run. Whew! I am so thankful my blinders were cracked open to see the problems before the situation became irreparable. The "worm" reared its ugly head, but thankfully it was in time!

The Danger of the Fast Track

Fortunately for me, the Lord's "A" team swooped in and rescued me from the situation; however, not everyone is so lucky.

Remember the joke, "What's worse than biting into an apple and finding a worm?" Answer: "Finding half a worm." I have a friend who took the fast track when it came to picking out the man with whom she thought she would spend the rest of her life. She is very cute, incredibly funny, loves the Lord wholeheartedly, and has an all-around great personality, which translated to a healthy number of consistent dates. Since she had such a steady flow of rendezvous, desperation was not really in play. Now, like most of us, a large majority of her friends were married or on their way down the aisle, so although waiting wasn't necessarily her strong suit, settling for someone mediocre was not in her plans.

She did all the right things, like keeping herself pure for her future mate and sincerely trusting God's sovereignty for her. Then she met "him." He appeared to be Mr. Perfect. He was tall, attractive, smart, and knew all the right things to say. Convinced she had found her soul mate in her newfound beau (which was largely due to circumstances that would present themselves later) they sped along the "love autobahn" together and were engaged within two weeks of meeting. (Wow, huh!) The whirlwind romance led to a six-month engagement before the union of their lives.

I wish for their sake the fairy tale was still playing out, complete with the happy ending. Instead, the report is a little bleaker. What she landed was not Mr. Wonderful but rather a wolf in sheep's clothing! My friend endured nearly a decade in a miserable marriage to a man she did not even know. She bit into her life's apple and discovered there was half a worm missing, the other half already in her belly! Gulp!

I could dedicate pages to how she (and he) made numerous efforts to make the marriage survive. I could spend hours justifying the end result of divorce, with notes from pastors and counselors, but it all goes back to the beginning . . . not the outcome.

Now keep in mind, this is a good woman who loves Jesus, her kids, and her family, and who never in a million years thought she would wear the *D* of divorcée. When she met and married her husband, she really thought it was forever. After all, they were in love! She sought what she comprehended was the Lord's will and undoubtedly presented the request before Him. But now, years later, my dear, sweet friend finds herself in the role of single mom to two great kids. And while God is blessing her and truly being a Husband to the husbandless and a Father to the fatherless, she still walks a path she would not wish on her worst enemy.

Now granted, my pal would surely agree that if she knew then what she knows now, she certainly would have taken some other road. What person who has walked the path of divorce wouldn't? The ancient proverb states that hindsight is 20/20, after all. However, the biggest lesson I continue to learn from her is summed up in something Edward Moore said in his work *The Happy Marriage:* "Time still, as he flies, brings increase to her truth." Granted, her time and truth are very different from mine, as she can't walk around defending her reputation and fighting every battle that may exist over her divorce. She has to let time exonerate her life through her own walk with the Lord. But as difficult as it has been watching her cling to that little piece of reality, I know that I need to understand and apply that on the front end of all my relationships, because I regularly open my heart too early on, only to walk away wounded from my own ignorance. Yes, it's undeniable that truth and time walk hand in hand.

TIME WILL TELL

Going back to my friend's situation, the problems did not begin after they were married—they just came to light then. Since their courtship was so incredibly short, there was no time to allow the truth to surface. The ultimate cause of their unfortunate divorce would have more than likely presented itself given more time to "get to know each other," undoubtedly preventing the doomed marriage in the first place. In the end, the emotional "love" they felt those first few months was not enough to sustain them for a lifetime, since the truth of who they each were was not based upon the time testing of reality. Character was not fully displayed before the decision to marry was made. Once she discovered whom she had married, it was too late to change the course without a nasty detour. See, godly character is demonstrated over time and through a myriad of circumstances; it's not a cheap display that one can simply fake. True character will be revealed; it's just a matter of how long it will take. It's been said that you can fool anyone for a year. (I didn't say it, so take it for what it's worth.) That's not the magic answer, but it should give you some idea of how long the "checking for worms" phase should last.

I believe the best application comes from the depiction of Ruth and Boaz's relationship in Scripture. First, you can't help but love Ruth's heart. To grasp the outcome, you need just a little background: Naomi is the mother-in-law, and Ruth and Orpah are married to her two boys. When all three of their husbands eventually die, there are choices to be made. Ruth 1:16–17 records Ruth's decision to step outside her comfort zone, relinquish her family and all she knows, and simply to be loyal to her bitter (Ruth 1:20) mother-in-law. Her sister-in-law, Orpah, jumped at the first offer of release offered by Naomi and was out of there with little else mentioned. Ruth sacrificed what she knew and chose to remain faithful. It is Ruth's words and subsequent action that display her character loud and clear.

The thing I love about this story is Ruth's and Boaz's prime examples of character. You can almost replay the scene over in your mind like a movie. Ruth stuck by her word, and when she and Naomi finally settled in her stepmother's chosen land, she dutifully went to work gleaning from Boaz's fields to feed herself and Naomi. If we pull back and look at the bigger picture of this little book, we can see all the signs that Boaz was watching her from afar. He set up protection and "purposefully" left a little extra in the fields for her; but more so, I can see him testing the strength of her character, which is where the real lesson lies. Truth and time walk hand in hand. A person's character is tested and tried over time. Even though Boaz was a kinsman redeemer to Naomi's husband, Elimelech, he was not in a rush to fulfill his rightful duties. (Essentially, a kinsman redeemer's role was to "buy back" or rescue the family or wife whose husband had died or left, and to claim any inheritance.)

Behind the Scenes

Even so, Boaz was taking care of Ruth behind the scenes, which speaks volumes about his character. He had his eye on her while she went about diligently working to survive. When Ruth finally went to lie at his feet, Boaz had obviously done his homework by checking to see just who Ruth was in her "downtime." Then he said,

> Blessed are you of the LORD, my daughter! For you have shown more kindness at the end than at the beginning, in that you did not go after young men, whether poor or rich. And now, my daughter, do not fear. I will do for you all that you request, for all the people of my town know that you are a virtuous woman. (Ruth 3:10–11 NKJV)

Boaz had gotten the report from all the city. Her character was time-tested and confirmed by a whole metropolis!

Like Boaz and Ruth, test all your relationships with time. If and when you finally marry, don't you consciously want to be happy with your choice for a mate (for longer than the honeymoon)? The reality is, the decisions we make today influence our "available" choices for tomorrow. Don't you think it would behoove you and me both, right now, to mindfully make the decision not to be desperate or needy, choosing to follow through with the testing of time to ensure the success of marriage?

I'm not trying to over-spiritualize the process, but the buck stops here. If we don't desire and choose those things now, what are we lining ourselves up for? Because, quite honestly, there are some days we are frustrated and tired of being alone, and we run to what is comfortable or *feels* good instead of what *is* good. I know. I am walking the path with you. I am very aware that there are days we want to be a mom and days we want to be loved and appreciated by someone tangible and present with "skin on." There are even days when, despite the truth, all of a sudden a past relationship that ended because of complete and total incompatibility doesn't look so bad. But I know God's best for me will come with His timing, and I would rather have a relationship like that of Boaz and Ruth than like those of miserable friends and relatives.

Don't misinterpret what I'm saying. I'm not pronouncing that you have to date for five years before you make the plunge. I'm not sure there really is any set amount of time to be friends before you start dating and no pat answers on when you need to get married after that process has been lived out. It's all on a case-by-case basis. However, what you do need to do is be patient enough to allow time to reveal true character. Because you know what? There really is little worse than getting a mouthful containing rotten fruit or half a worm. Trust me, save yourself the heartache!

⁕

Now you are saying something! What is it about a woman? She can commit her heart without using her head. Would you buy a house without checking out the interior? I don't think so! Yet many women go for the pretty house (as in cute man) only to find out later there is nobody home. Or nobody they want to live with anyway. If you've read any of my other books, such as *Secrets of an Irresistible Woman* or *If Men Are Like Buses Then How Do I Catch One?* where I go into great detail on this subject, you know what I have to say about that. Slow down, Sally! Dating is not for mating, it is for collecting data to see if the person even *qualifies* for courtship before you start trying on peau de soie pumps.

The last time I broke this rule, it ended in disaster—or should I say it *could* have ended in disaster if I had given my heart away. I was still trying to decide how I felt about the person when they revealed their hand, and it was ugly. However, the scary part of this whole thing was that all my friends and those close to me were sold on him. He was a Christian; his passion was for prayer and the arts. He went on mission trips at least twice a year. He was an incredible con-versationalist and cu-ute! Kinda looked like Val Kilmer. The total dream package. He thought I was the best thing since sliced bread. He celebrated my gifts. He was romantic . . . Let me give you an example, because he took romance to another level, and I want you to see how slick the devil can be if you're not watching.

Too Good to Be True

This man went to Africa on a missions trip, and I expected not to hear from him until he came back to America two weeks later, because he was going to be in some rather remote villages. Well, the day after he arrived I got a phone call from him. He informed me he had been able to pay someone there to let him use their satellite phone to call me. Then he said, "Michelle, it is so incredible here. I'm surrounded by at least a hundred children with drums in this little village, and I've asked them to play for you . . ." On that note, he held out the phone and said, "All right, you can play now!" And the children began drumming and singing to me over the phone! From *Africa*, okay?! Yes, go ahead and bite your knuckles. I did.

That was just one example of his sense of romance and the types of things he did to woo me. He was perfect. Remember that rule about if it looks too good to be true, it probably is? Well, there you have it. I carefully proceeded in prayer, because actually I was terrified that he was the one and wanted to make sure before I flew into a commitment-phobic panic. And then I had the oddest dream, in which I came upon him all covered up, not looking like himself at all. When I pulled back the rags, he was filthy and deformed. I woke up and pondered what God was trying to tell me. I soon found out when, after praying and asking God to remove him if he wasn't the one for me, this wonderful man vanished into thin air without an explanation. Yes, I mean vanished! Never to be heard from again for an entire year and a half. He then sent a brief note apologizing for his behavior, citing that it was wrong of him and asking for forgiveness. I never replied. I decided to let sleeping dogs lie.

Now you're probably wondering, *Didn't you call him, Michelle?* Well, I called him once—after my mother said I should check to see if anything had happened to him. You see, our parting words that last conversation were the agreement that he was to pray and seek God concerning where our relationship should go. I told him to take his time, I was in no hurry. Initially when I didn't hear from him I assumed he was still talking to God, and I didn't want to interrupt the conversation. After about a month I called and left a voice mail, inquiring if he was all right. When I didn't get a reply, I released him. Of course I was angry and upset with how he had handled the situation, but God reminded me that I had asked Him to remove the man if his intentions toward me were not right. I had to accept that, and I moved on.

What were the rules I broke? I didn't gather enough data. He lived in another state, and I was not privy to seeing him in his environment, meeting his friends or family. I had no history on him other than what he supplied. People cloak themselves in mystery for a reason. In the end I received a few trickles of information from a friend who lived near him and had stumbled across an acquaintance of his. This woman informed my friend that though he seemed to be quite vocal about his faith, he appeared to have commitment issues and had broken several engagements with other women. The last time she had seen him in a social setting he had been drinking excessively . . . Whew! You could have knocked me over with a feather. This is not the image he had painted for me at all.

The Moral of the Story

Don't get excited about the cover until you read the contents. When in doubt, ask God to show you the fine print. He who knows every man's heart and searches them will not keep you in the dark about anything or anyone. He will reveal secrets and issues to you about the person you are considering, even in the midnight hour. He had shown me in my dream that this man was hiding something and was unclean or had unclean motives toward me. He rescued me from certain distress. If you truly trust God and believe that He knows what is best for you, it is imperative that you allow Him to separate the men from the boys in your life. Allow Him to counsel you concerning them, and take His advice when He points out the red flags and caution signs.

Most important, give Him a free hand to remove anyone from your life who is not good for you. Remember that He promises to give us "good and perfect" gifts. Psalm 84:11 says, "No good thing will He withhold from those who walk uprightly" (NKJV). If that is the case, rest in the fact that if a man is good for you, he will be yours; but if he is not, he will be removed. Rejoice in the fact that God's prevention is His ultimate protection of your heart, and purpose to wait for nothing less than the best for you. Just remember, what *looks* good to you may not always be good *for* you!

16 I Knew I Loved You Before I Met You, but You're Driving Me Crazy!

The steps of a good man are ordered by the Lord, and He delights in his way.

—PSALM 37:23 NKJV

My mom and I recently took a vacation together to Europe. While I was content to stay in Paris, my mother proposed that since we were going all that way, we should visit the other half of the free world while we were in the neighborhood. Needless to say (and against my better judgment), I agreed to the idea to visit six additional countries. So with everything settled, we prepared for the expedition. We had maps, AAA travel books, worship CDs, and our adventuresome spirits.

Day three into our journey we wandered out to the Charles de Gaulle Airport in Paris, France, and picked up our rental car. Now, first off, driving overseas is a little different from the get-go. I should have known we'd experienced only the beginning of craziness when the first questions were: "Do you want air-conditioning?" And my personal favorite, "Would you like manual or automatic transmission madamoiselle?" You know, things that are considered "no-brainers" here. (Yes, we got air but were not so lucky on the automatic transmission, in case you were wondering. And yes, it was an extraordinary pain in the Swiss Alps!)

The Best-Laid Plans of Mice and Men

After sorting out a mini reservation fiasco (which took nearly an hour to correct), we hit the highway. Everything was going as planned until we got into Luxembourg, where we discovered the maps we had brought along were very generalized. We had about eight maps floating around the car, so we thought we had everything we could possibly need. Not so! (Just FYI . . . AAA does not have all the answers overseas which I should have clued in by the *American* Automobile Association title). It was late afternoon (a.k.a. rush hour) when we hit the grand duchy capital city with a map that showed gray blobs where roads and landmarks should have been. Couple that with the fact that I had a bifocal-wearing copilot who wasn't able to read the map without her glasses, let alone shift her focus immediately to the signs ahead. The signs, written in three languages, were whipping past us faster than we could keep up. Uh-oh . . . now there was a big problem! Two American women in a foreign land armed with a stick-shift wagon, bent bifocals, and bad maps. Gulp—watch out!

Unfortunately, their roadways are considerably different from ours in most every way. Who would have thought it'd be so different halfway around the world? (Duh, Holly!) The most obvious difference, of course, is speed. (But remember, I had a Renault station wagon, not a Lamborghini.) In the States, once you are on a highway, you are on there until you get off at an exit or you hit another highway. We soon discovered it doesn't work like that over there. We would be on a "highway" and then the main passageway would go right into the middle of town complete with stoplights, bumper-to-bumper traffic, and forty-five-kilometer-an-hour speed limits.

Icing the cake, the roadways were not clearly or well marked. As you can imagine, we drove around aimlessly for a while, finally stopped and asked for directions, drove some more, stopped and asked for directions again, and eventually found our way out of the city to the highway, only to repeat the scene in the next major metropolis of Brussels. Our overall problem was that we just did not have all the necessary information. A country map with a city surrounded in gray was not the best choice for the situation. If we would have had detailed information of the city streets, we would have known, for example, that the highway picked up twelve blocks down instead of trusting the confusing roadway signs. Our assumption that a highway was a highway mislead us.

Too often we rush into a relationship having only a "generalized map" and assuming that we know where we are going. We speed out of the parking lot, excited about the adventure but lacking the detailed information needed to navigate the relationship effectively. All the signs are pointing to what we think is the right direction. Too often we've misread them, though, and we end up lost and confused, needing to find new directions. We get lost, lose our tempers, have our hearts broken, and waste too much time and energy driving in circles. Once we get there, we realize the destination was not at all worth the arduous and long trip. (Nothing against Luxembourg; to each his own.)

When we are courting or dating, you can bet that we are

functioning in a world of misinformation and half-truths. Without so much as another thought, I purposely suppress my temper, dress a little snazzier, and lower my voice to be more demure. God only knows that the men are fighting urges to clean their ears with their car keys or not pick their noses while we are looking, and reportedly the toughest of all . . . remembering to wash their hands after a visit to the rest room. A good date is conscious to present their best side, to put their best foot forward. It's just a part of the process, but the information is definitely different with closer inspection.

A Shangri-la

Anyone who is (or has been) married can tell you that the mapped destination of perfect harmony does not exist, but we still expect to find and dwell in the imaginary Shangri-la. For myself, the daunting task of realistically creating in my mind the ideal mate seemed harsh and somewhat unrealistic. Generating a perfect man in an imperfect world seemed to establish some kind of impossible standard I would never find. I mentioned accusations of being too picky earlier because of my selectivity in the past, but nowadays I say to that . . . yes, I am—so what? I refuse to settle for just any warm body (that surely is a sign of maturity, right?).

Though I always thought I'd know when it was right, I am coming to a place in my life where I no longer trust my instincts or assumptions. For this reason, I have basically created a "plumb line" to follow when I lose my head. (You know it happens, don't act so innocent!) The evaluation starts with a list of ten "must-have" character traits that are important to me, which I determined while I was levelheaded and thinking clearly (in other words, now). For example, I selected godliness as the most important character trait and rank a potential mate's godliness by what I can perceive from the outside.

Keep in mind, there is a fine line between judgment and evaluation, so be cautious of how you rank people, and know you may be ranked on a similar level. "Do not judge, or you too will be judged. For in the same way you judge others, you will be judged, and with the measure you use, it will be measured to you" (Matt. 7:1–2 NIV). Be fair and realistic.

If I rate someone a 7 out of 10, that's a C by most standards. Do I want to marry someone who rates a C in this category? Will I be happy with that score, or will I eventually become frustrated if they never improve their grade? Most people will not change a significant amount and the older in age, the less likely they are to change. So at least by giving them a 6 in sensitivity, I realize what I would be getting into ahead of time. Does it meet my plumb-line standard? Essentially, what I am doing is drawing out a road map and charting directions. I am familiarizing myself with the territory to see if the journey (dating/courting) is worth the destination (marriage).

Here is the grading scale most of us have grown up with. It is simple enough for you to translate this scale over to our ratings.

A	9–10	90–100
B	8	80
C	7	70
D	6	60
F	5 or less	50 or below

In order to "rank" the things that are important to you in a godly mate, choose the top ten characteristics you would like your mate to possess (in an ideal world), then give each characteristic a beginning score potential of 10 points. Now adjust the weight each trait carries to reflect its importance to you. As I mentioned, the top trait on my chart is godliness. In order for that trait to carry more weight, I'm going to double it and make it be worth 20 points. If you choose to double points on certain traits, it may be necessary for you to drop a trait that is relatively insignificant so say now you only have 9 traits for instance. You can assign the score potential however you wish, as long as at the end you have a total potential scoring of 100.

The next thing you need to do is jump over to the last column, and select, based on what you know you desire right now, what your pass or fail minimums are. For instance, in the first trait of godliness, I cannot, for my own good, settle for anyone who scores below 14 out of the 20 I've assigned, or in other words below a C. I feel that in assigning that score, I allow for potential and avoid judgment; however, the man's role as spiritual leader is an important item to me. I desire someone who will be spiritually in tune to that role without coaxing or begging.

This is a good evaluation to use when you begin to date someone. If they rank low, offer grace for improvement and set a realistic amount of time before you reevaluate to see if they were just having a rough patch. Keep in mind, however, that based on your "needs," they may not be the absolute best one out there for you. If you have your "fail-safe" in place, that keeps you accountable to a standard. If you choose to disregard your minimum requirements, it will, at the least, allow you to process a second look, and the foresight to be aware of potential issues before they could become a problem.

The example on the next page shows eight traits with the points adjusted to reflect the preferences of the ranker against their perception of the person they are rating.

Character Trait	Score Potential	Actual Score	Letter Grade	Pass/Fail Minimum
Godliness	20	16	B	14
Honesty	15	12	B	9
Humor	15	13	B	9
Intelligence	10	6	D	4
Attractiveness	10	2	F	3
Sensitivity	10	4	F	4
Personality	10	7	C	7
Work Ethic	10	9	A	7
	100	69		

Now in the example above, Joe Blow is pretty decent catch. The only thing he didn't pass was attractiveness . . . can I wash that? Probably so, but be it one of the others I'd have to think twice about it. Set your own traits for your ideal mate, and use the following blank chart to score the person in your life.

Character Trait	Score Potential	Actual Score	Letter Grade	Pass/Fail Minimum
	100			

This works for me because I know that I need accountability in my life, a standard I can go back to. None of us are perfect, least of all me, and I know firsthand that it is hard to judiciously and without bias sort out emotions and feelings when you finally meet someone. It's easy to adopt the "He's here, so he must be right" mentality, but we ultimately know what we want in life and in the person we share it with. Sadly enough, our fears of being alone often drive us into the arms of the wrong person, adjusting those mental notes to compensate.

Just as in traveling it's a good idea to know the route and have detailed maps of your destination before you get on the journey, it's smart to take the time to do a little research and understand a relationship before rushing into a commitment you can neither keep nor desire. There are some "deal-breakers" that might not seem to matter at first, but they will pile up fast!

I knew I loved Europe before I even got on the road, but the map fiasco really affected my level of enjoyment! I wasn't adequately prepared for what I would encounter on the trip and was ultimately frustrated by the situation. Now, every trip I make, I carefully research, obtain maps, and plan ahead, getting *all* the details so I don't make the same mistakes. Gray-blobbed maps are discarded and replaced with intricate city maps. How much more cautious we need to be in regard to the one we'll give ourselves to!

⌒

Truly, men are like a foreign country. You might know the signs in female country for when to slow down, turn left or right in a conversation, or just stop where you are, but the signs don't translate when you apply them to men. They are a different species. That's why advice from other women doesn't work well when you're trying to figure out a man. This is where male friends come in handy. They will tell you what to look for, when to let them slide, and when to push the eject button.

However, the Holy Spirit is always the best instructor on these matters. It's good to have a list and a grading system as a working outline for basic requirements, but you still won't have all the facts you need to work with. He who searches the heart of man and knows the mind of the Spirit of God will still need to be consulted. A good man can look bad depending on when you cross his path. The Holy Spirit can give you insight into the hidden things. Always adhere to the non-negotiables, such as "must have a relationship with God," "can't be a serial killer," etc. But when in doubt ask the Holy Spirit for sound counsel. Also seek the counsel of older women who have successful relationships. Notice the requirements. Never ask someone for advice if they have not accomplished what you are trying to do. There is a reason they haven't if it is simply not an issue of God's timing or purpose at work in their lives.

I know that it is because of the call of God on my life that I am not married yet, though I could have been several times. When it comes to giving advice on how to live a productive and joyful single life, I am an expert. But when seeking advice in relationships with men, I seek the counsel of successful married women or happy single women who stick to the Word and not to their personal opinions, which may be laden with personal baggage. Proceed with caution, pay attention to the signs, and be ready for unexpected twists and turns.

The Road Less Paved

The road to love is not smooth. You must be ready for the journey and have enough gas to stay on the road for a time, because it's hard to tell when you will arrive at your destination. Remember the foolish virgins? They missed the wedding because they were not sufficiently prepared to wait for the bridegroom. Oops upside your head! Getting past weariness and not settling for a rest stop is half the battle. That's when we get in trouble—when we're feeling as if we're lost or we're never going to reach Oz. Anybody starts looking good to you. You start thinking, *Well, if I clean him up and dress him up, he'll do.* Wake up. He'll only "do" for the first week of marriage, if that long. Consider the fact that those who fall deeply in love with their husbands still find something about them they can't stand after living with them for a while. If the person you marry is only someone you settled for, you are going to find a multitude of things you can't stand about him later.

Beyond the non-negotiables, are there any rules for the sort of man you should be looking for? Not really. It becomes completely subjective. Every woman dreams of the wealthy prince who will come and carry her away from the trials of paying the bills, living on a limited income and having to handle everything in her life. Of owning a fabulous house and living the life of Riley, traveling to exotic places and having the perfect marriage. What a state of utopia that would be! But alas and alack, it is only a dream. There are only so many wealthy men around, and usually they are looking for women who have money, too. Yes, you have to be what you want to attract. Birds of a feather flock together, and *Pretty Woman* is a just a movie.

Living the American Dream

Keep in mind that the American (or is it worldwide?) dream comes with its own set of headaches. Wealthy, high-powered husbands are usually more busy than their wives really like.

After all, they are busy being wealthy and high-powered! You still need a life of your own—your own sense of purpose—to fill in the blanks. This usually throws women for a loop. What happened to the romance, the impromptu European trips, and picnics in the park? Honey, that is simply not real life. Real life makes it necessary to do some things you don't always enjoy. Working to pay for all that you acquire. It's doing what you have to do to meet your obligations.

Mate selection must be based on what you know you need as opposed to what you think you want. The two can be poles apart. Do you want a good man who is grounded, hardworking, and simply loves you? Then he might not come in the flashy package that you like. However, he might be a better candidate for fulfilling your heart's desire. Yes, you must become realistic about your expectations and the choices you make.

Choosing character over surface luster will bring longer-lasting benefits to your life.

Consider that there was nothing flashy about Jesus as He walked the streets of Nazareth, yet He was a King in disguise. Don't overlook that nice, quiet man; take the time to discover that still waters run deep. That man who is delightful but looks kind of nerdy? Hey, that's a haircut and a change of clothing. Don't throw out the baby with the bathwater. Look for the king inside; the outer package can be rearranged.

Still think you have to have the picture-perfect model? My final recommendation is to keep your standards, but also keep an open mind and give God the go-ahead to surprise you. More often than not God doesn't send you what you're expecting, but something even better than what you had in mind, though you might not initially recognize it as such. Every woman who is extremely happy in her marriage has uttered the same words: "He wasn't the man I expected, but he is everything that I wanted. I sure am glad I stepped past my expectations and listened to the Lord." Truly, the Lord is the best matchmaker! He is able to weave our dreams with our needs and present them in a package that will make us squeal with delight.

17 True Confessions: Head-to-Head with Michelle and Holly

Well, Michelle, we finally made it to the end. I'm not sure what we have left to cover. I know we've always joked about what our last goals were before the Lord came back, and mine are spiritual and yours are physical, but how's that translate into one last chapter? Do you think we left out anything?

Did we tell them to get a life?

Yeah, we told them that.

Did we tell them that getting married isn't the answer?

Yep.

Did we tell them if their spiritual life isn't together their social life won't be either?

Pretty sure we did. But you know, there are going to be some people who just don't get it, even after everything we've written here. We've bared our souls, but they need something more . . .

I know; it just takes time for some people. There are a couple of prerequisites to being able to receive what we have to say. First of all, you have to be at the end of yourself. You have to have tried every other way around God's Word and found it to fail, looked for love in all the wrong places and come up empty-handed. Finally, you need to be at the place where you are sick and tired of being sick and tired. The smart ones will listen to good advice, while others will have to exhaust the full journey of learning things the hard way.

Then, and pretty much only then, will they be ready to hear what we've been saying. Until that time, they need to put this book on the shelf and leave it there. When they finally come around and are willing to try something new, they need to revisit it. I love the maxim that says, "Until the pain of staying the same is greater than the pain of change, we won't change." The bottom line is that doing the same thing never gets you different results.

I hear that! I couldn't stand to sit still while life passed me by! I learned early enough on that I can make a heaven out of hell or a hell out of heaven. I work hard and I play hard. If it's a money thing, I'll just make more. If I want to do it, I'll scrimp and save and make it happen. If it's a time issue, I'll carve it out somehow. But in all seriousness, Michelle, when did all this click in for you? You've got fifteen years on me, but how long did it take you to get to the place where you are living what we've been saying?

Girl, it seemed like forever, but let's just say it took me long enough. Trust me, I broke all the rules. Frank Sinatra and I were twins because I, too, "did it my way." I went to all the wrong places, was attracted to all the wrong faces, loved all the wrong men, got my heart broke, and turned around and did it again.

There's only so many times you can tape a raggedy heart back together before you realize you're only damaging yourself by refusing to let go and let God take the wheel because, obviously, you don't know how to drive. So I have to say, I'm very passionate about what I teach now because I know the results of the alternative firsthand.

Michelle, what about those people who "get" only part of the book. They agree with some concepts but drop the rest of them?

Well, then they'll only get half the results. It's as if they're asking, "How much can I sin before it's actually considered sin? If I'm just a little stupid, will I be considered completely stupid?"

Along the lines of there is some dirt in the brownies, but only a little dirt . . . how many do you want? Duh, none, there's dirt in there!

Yes, there comes a point in time when you have to look at the big picture of your life and decide what you want to see there. You've got to come to a decision about what you'll be proud to hang on the wall. Also, what will it take to complete a picture that you'll want others to view? It has to involve planning and careful selection of your color palette. Though other colors may distract you, you've got to stick to the color scheme of the life you are painting. This calls for discipline and keeping the end picture in mind to create the masterpiece called your life. Life doesn't just happen. Love doesn't just happen. The decisions you make shape the outcome of both. At some point, we have to grow up and decide how we want to shape our existence.

I'm apparently still mixing my colors, dipping in some other shades to add some flair, but I have the concept down. When did that happen for you?

It happened one day when I got up and I realized I had been depressed for a very long time. As a matter of fact, I couldn't remember the last time I had truly been happy. I realized I had lost control of my world and had allowed myself to be controlled by too many foolish choices and circumstances. It was then that I opened my hands and gave God the reins of my life. I chose to submit to His Word, no matter how uncomfortable it was for me initially.

I did that, too, but I found that I kept snatching back control. Did you ever take the reins back from God?

Oh, sure . . . we fought over them for a while. However, the longer I did things His way, the more I realized I had actually been doing things the hard way before. His yoke *was* easy; His burden *was* light! I felt like, duh, I should have had a V-8. What's the song say? "O what needless pain we bear, all because we do not carry everything to God in prayer." That about summed it up for me.

I know I'm a little unorthodox in my approach, as you are in yours, but what did you learn by writing this book with me, Michelle?

That it's easy to slip back into old patterns and mind-sets if you don't stay focused on where you're going. I suppose I'm so passionate about sharing the message of hope with singles because I know the depth of their misery; I've been there. I've also been a victim of the deceptive thinking that says it's not possible for life to get any better.

And if you had it to do over again, you'd no doubt avoid it.

Oh, of course. If I had only known then what I know now, I could have been enjoying life a whole lot sooner, because the bottom line is this: It *is* possible to be single and extremely happy.

So are you telling me that you don't care what the return policy is?

I'm telling you there are a lot of returns for living the life you're living, *if* you're exercising all the options and taking advantage of all God offers. The secret to successful single living is not just being interested in someone and having someone, but being interested in life, period.

So not necessarily taking singleness back to "trade in" for marriage, but rather recognizing that it is a very valuable gift with lots of benefits. Essentially, using the gift effectively until the trade is natural or until this gift wears out and needs replacing. That it is imperative to being well-rounded and based in Christ.

Uh-huh, yep. That's what makes you interesting.

So Michelle, lay it all out. Bottom-line it for me here.

Just remember that purpose comes first, partner second. However, it's the purpose that puts you in position to receive the right partner. When Adam got busy doing his assignment in the garden, God decided he needed help to complete his mission. You don't need help feeling sorry for yourself. So if that's where you are, you'll remain there until you choose a different path. The wonderful thing about choice is, God has given us the power to choose. So stop volunteering for misery and loneliness. Choose joy on purpose. Make a decision to do whatever is necessary to make your life the type of life you enjoy living.

People have told me (and I'm sure you, too) that they wish they had my life, it seems so glamorous—all the traveling, performing, and hanging out with "famous" people. What advice do you have for them?

That's impossible. Everyone has to make their own life.

Right, and we've worked hard to reach the level of joy that we have. But what's a one-line answer for them?

Above all things, choose to love the Lover of your soul with unadulterated fervor.

That's it! Anything else you want to add?

I'm done. I don't know what else I can say. I've got a date with a rich old Jewish Man. So, I'll end my dissertation and get to it!

If you already know Christ but have been struggling with your singleness, we hope we have offered you something that will broaden your approach to living the single life more joyfully. Taking up your cross and dying daily doesn't sound like the most fun thing to do. However, the more you surrender, the more you stand to gain. If you do not know about Christ, then you actually have a copy of this book in your hands for one basic reason: You really aren't ready to live until you are ready to die. This book is written from the perspectives of two Christian women who have made every effort to offer you tried and true godly solutions and biblical teaching. If you don't know for sure whether you will spend eternity in heaven or in hell, then it's important that we give you the details.

PUT IT IN PERSPECTIVE

If a stewardess on a flight hands you a parachute "because it will give you a more comfortable ride," sooner or later you will come to the realization that it is anything but comfortable, and you will remove it because it isn't doing what she said it would do. However, if the attendant says, "Put on the parachute. This plane is going to crash soon, and you will need it to save your life," you will not care that it is uncomfortable or that others laugh. You will keep it on because you know in the end that parachute is going to save your life.

The above example parallels the way we may view Christ's free gift to us. Accepting Christ as your Savior doesn't mean you'll be worry-free or that you'll never have anything bad happen to you again. It might even be "uncomfortable" at times. But there is a very real force named Satan battling for souls even as you read this. Hell and Satan are tangible and real, as are God and heaven. If you accept this "parachute," it will save your soul. A decision needs to be made, and by not making one, you confirm your choice of hell.

This is so much bigger than whom you will marry, where you live, or what you do for a living. We are dealing with eternity, which is impossible to grasp. It is a decision that only you can make. You must discover Him and the truths for yourself. I have tried to make it as easy as I can for you to generate an educated and informed decision in the following pages full of Scriptures. You can explore them and read the context surrounding them.

Last, the verdict you declare has to be made in your heart. Choosing Christ so that you will merely have "fire insurance" is not how it works. But as the foundation of the biggest perk ever known, it's good to know that's certainly a top benefit!

The Bible says, "For if you confess with your mouth that Jesus is Lord and believe in your heart that God raised him from the dead, you will be saved" (Rom. 10:9 NLT). It's as easy as believing that. Here is a prayer you can pray in your own heart. It will help you in your decision to receive Christ as your Savior.

> Lord, I know that I am a sinner and deserve punishment. Please forgive me. My sins have separated me from You. I believe that You sent Your Son, Jesus, to die on the cross for my sins, and I believe that after His crucifixion You raised Him from the dead to bear the burden of all my wrongs. I ask You, Jesus, to become my personal Savior. In simple faith I ask that You come into my heart and save me. Amen.

If you prayed this prayer with sincerity, God has promised to save you. "For whosoever shall call upon the name of the Lord shall be saved" (Rom. 10:13 KJV). If you believed it in your heart, you have become a Christian and your name has been written in the Lamb's book of life. I know that it's hard to make a decision and not know exactly all it entails, so I encourage you to find a nearby place to worship and fellowship and begin reading the Bible, starting in the book of Matthew. I have also included an appendix at the end of the book that contains selected Scriptures for you to study on confirming your decision.

Please write to let us know of your decision so we can send you a Bible or some materials to help you learn more. We'd love to hear from you!

Holly Virden
Segue Media
P.O. Box 1887
Brentwood, TN 37024-1887
holly@hollyvirden.com

Michelle McKinney Hammond
Heartwing Ministries
P.O. Box 11052
Chicago, IL 60611
www.mckinneyhammond.com
heartwingmin@yahoo.com

To Book Holly or Michelle for Speaking Engagements:

Segue Media
877-240-0712

Speak Up Speaker Services
888-870-7719

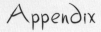Appendix

God's Plan of Salvation: How to Know You'll Spend Eternity in Heaven

THE BIBLE SAYS:

I. The entire world of mankind has sinned. That includes you and it includes me.

- "For all have sinned, and come short of the glory of God" (Rom. 3:23 KJV).
- "But the Scriptures have declared that we are all prisoners of sin, so the only way to receive God's promise is to believe in Jesus Christ" (Gal. 3:22 NLT).
- "As it is written, There is none righteous, no, not one" (Rom. 3:10 KJV).
- "There is not a single person in all the earth who is always good and never sins" (Eccl. 7:20 NLT).

II. Jesus Christ became a sacrifice for your sin upon the cross. God placed all your sin upon His only Son, Jesus Christ. As your sacrifice, Jesus paid for the penalty of your sin, which was hell. He also died to forgive you of all sin, which separated you from God. Through His sacrifice on the cross, you can have your sins forgiven, be rescued from hell, and be restored to Him.

- "For I delivered unto you first of all that which I also received, how that Christ died for our sins according to the scriptures" (1 Cor. 15:3 KJV).
- "But God showed his great love for us by sending Christ to die for us while we were still sinners" (Rom. 5:8 NLT).
- "Christ also suffered when he died for our sins once for all time. He never sinned, but he died for sinners that he might bring us safely home to God. He suffered physical death, but he was raised to life in the Spirit" (1 Peter 3:18 NLT).
- "If that had been necessary, he would have had to die again and again, ever since the world began. But no! He came once for all time, at the end of the age, to remove the power of sin forever by his sacrificial death for us" (Heb. 9:26 NLT).
- "He personally carried away our sins in his own body on the cross so we can be dead to sin and live for what is right. You have been healed by his wounds!" (1 Peter 2:24 NLT).

III. Jesus Christ rose from the grave to show that God the Father accepted His offering for our sin upon the cross. Christ rose from the dead so He could give you the salvation He provided on the cross. He is alive and wants to save you today. He can become your living, personal Savior from sin and hell.

- "He was buried, and he was raised from the dead on the third day, as the Scriptures said" (1 Cor. 15:4 NLT).
- "For if you confess with your mouth that Jesus is Lord and believe in your heart that God raised him from the dead, you will be saved" (Rom. 10:9 NLT).
- "He was handed over to die because of our sins, and he was raised from the dead to make us right with God" (Rom. 4:25 NLT).

IV. Man can get to God and heaven only through the Lord

Jesus Christ. No idol, person, priest, religion, or good deeds will give you access or acceptance before God. Man has attempted to save himself from hell and restore his favor to a Holy God by doing good works, going to church, and obeying certain commands. The Bible says all of our human works will not save us, but only through God's grace and forgiveness seen in the death and resurrection of Christ.

- "Jesus saith unto him, I am the way, the truth, and the life: no man cometh unto the Father, but by me" (John 14:6 KJV).
- "For there is one God, and one mediator between God and men, the man Christ Jesus" (1 Tim. 2:5 KJV).
- "Neither is there salvation in any other: for there is none other name under heaven given among men, whereby we must be saved" (Acts 4:12 KJV).

V. You can have the forgiveness of sin and salvation from hell that Christ offers to you. By a definite act of faith (belief), trust Christ to be your Savior.

- "We are all infected and impure with sin. When we proudly display our righteous deeds, we find they are but filthy rags" (Isa. 64:6 NLT).
- "For by grace are ye saved through faith; and that not of yourselves: it is the gift of God: not of works, lest any man should boast" (Eph. 2:8–9 KJV).
- "Not by works of righteousness which we have done, but according to his mercy he saved us" (Titus 3:5 KJV).
- "But people are declared righteous because of their faith, not because of their work" (Rom. 4:5 NLT).

VI. Trusting Jesus means that you believe He will do what He has promised. He will save you. You must simply place faith (belief) in Christ as you would place faith in a doctor, dentist, or lawyer. The difference with belief in Jesus Christ is that Christ is the only Person who can save you. There must be a definite place and time when you truly do believe on Jesus Christ to be your Savior, just as there was a definite place and time when we were born into this world.

- "Believe on the Lord Jesus Christ, and thou shalt be saved" (Acts 16:31 KJV).
- "For by grace are ye saved through faith" (Eph. 2:8 KJV).
- "But as many as received him, to them gave he power to become the sons of God, even to them that believe on his name" (John 1:12 KJV).
- "For whosoever shall call upon the name of the Lord shall be saved" (Rom. 10:13 KJV).
- "Behold, now is the accepted time; behold, now is the day of salvation" (2 Cor. 6:2 KJV).

WOULD YOU LIKE TO BELIEVE ON JESUS CHRIST RIGHT NOW FOR THE FORGIVENESS OF YOUR SINS?

Christ lives within you.
- "Christ in you, the hope of glory" (Col. 1:27 KJV).

Christ has forgiven you of all your sins.
- "In whom we have redemption through his blood, even the forgiveness of sins" (Col. 1:14 KJV).

Christ has made you His child.
- "But as many as received him, to them gave he power to become the sons of God, even to them that believe on his name" (John 1:12 KJV).

Christ has given you eternal life.
- "Verily, verily, I say unto you, He that believeth on me hath everlasting life" (John 6:47 KJV); "The gift of God [Salvation] is eternal life" (Rom. 6:23 KJV).

Bibliography

Lucado, Max. *No Wonder They Call Him the Savior.* Sisters, Oreg.: Multnomah, 1986.

_____. *Traveling Light Journal.* Nashville, Tenn.: W Publishing Group, 2001.

Manning, Brennan. *The Ragamuffin Gospel.* Sisters, Oreg.: Multnomah, 1990.

Moore, Beth. *Praying God's Word.* Nashville, Tenn.: Broadman & Holman, 2000.

Piper, John. *Desiring God.* Sisters, Oreg.: Multnomah, 1996.

Holly Acknowledges...

All the praise, honor, and glory go to my Lord and King, Jesus Christ. He has poured out his blessings on my life so abundantly that my cup really does run over! This project has been a whirlwind of His grace, and I daily stand in awe of His goodness and blessings! Mom & Dad, thank you for loving me so well (and for making me well-rounded <wink>). I love you so much more than words can say! Gentry—you'll probably never read this book, but thanks for being a good baby brother. I love you. Michelle McKinney Hammond—girlfriend, I can't believe you! You continue to blow my mind, and I'm so thankful you're in my life! Thank you for catching my vision and for being my bud! I couldn't have done it without you (and wouldn't have wanted to)! You are amazing, and I thank the Lord for you every day! Let's shop, baby!

Thomas Nelson, for believing in this project and enabling our lives to reach out to other singles! My editors, Brian Hampton and Kyle Olund—my English teachers would like to thank you most of all . . . they know what a big job you had! Thanks for fixing my "lack of good English" traumas and my punctuation where I pause. Chip McGregor & my new friends at Alive Communications—thanks for believing in me, and thanks for all your hard work! Chip, your encouragement and guidance have spurred me on! Thanks for being there! David Garfinkle—for providing sound advice on all that "grown up" stuff. Thanks for working so hard on behalf of little ol' me. "Shannanay" Sparks— thanks for being my accountability partner, holding me to a higher standard on this project. I cherish our friendship and can't wait to see where our ministries will lead us. Thank you for standing with me and being the primary sounding board despite your crazy schedule! I love you!

Kim Hill—why, again, didn't we do this sooner? You're incredible! I appreciate your heart of worship and your sweet, sweet spirit! Thank you for entrusting your "life" to me and being so incredibly flexible while I "ignored" you to finish this. Lisa Harper—thanks for lending your infinite knowledge, unrestrained vocabulary, and, of course, your constant encouragement to me. Liz Curtis Higgs—thanks for sharing your "book" knowledge and teaching me to love myself. You are precious to me! Audrey Blanco, Karen Herbert and Bobbie Rill—my Women of Virtue girls, thanks for always cheering for me and getting me "gigs!" (Do I owe you commissions yet?) Thanks for ministering to my heart the past few years. I pray we have many more together!

The Green family—Bri and Wen . . . and you always thought you'd be the only one to give credits! Thanks for believing in me and trusting me so much early on in your ministry. Your encouragement in this season of my life has been invaluable. Coop and Gat—thanks for always being willing to play with Aunt Holly on a whim! I pray His will for you both daily! Susan Gray—I am so thankful to count you as a friend!

Pam and Dale See—true lifeguards! I am so thankful the Lord put you in my life even though now that I'm "grown up" (which is all subjective, of course) we don't see each other as often as I'd like. Tammy Lenderink—thanks for displaying to me that God is sovereign, even when we "don't get it." You da bomb, sistah! (Wanna work out?) The Rohn family—faithful friends who've stood the test of time. Steve and Shane Oakley—you are both a treasure! (I wasn't going 92!) My Thursday-night Bible study buddies—you gals are it! I take pleasure in our fellowship, and I love you all. Thanks for your prayer support throughout this project and in every little detail of my life! Yoda, Lori, Eric and Janie, Paul and Jeannine, and Todd and Michelle—Where on earth would I be without best friends like you guys? I love you bunches! Thanks for being constant and sturdy, especially when I've been irregular and weak in my "scheduling" time with you.

Pensacola Christian College—for teaching me that character is what you are when you are alone. Tom and Char Tucker, Andy and Linda Hamilton, Gerald and Bonnie Dufelmeier, Alan and Kaylene Bellmore, Gene and Sandy Howell, Scott and Jim Birkey, and a slew of others at Groveland Missionary Church. Your service and dedication to me when I was just beginning this journey in the Christian life is impossible to properly thank here on this earth. Through Missionary Cadets, Sunday School, Pioneer Clubs, and MYF, you were there showing me how to love Jesus through your life and teaching me what it really means to live for Christ. I can't thank you enough for investing your life into me. I adore and admire you all and count my blessings everyday that you are a part of my being! "Thank you" does not cover the depth of my appreciation, but alas, it's all I have for now. For all the people in my life that space will not allow a named mention, thank you for being my friends, family, and source of strength. You are special to me (even if I did run out of room to list you!)

Last, since He is the beginning and end of me, Jesus for being my all in all!

Michelle Acknowledges . . .

Holly, you know you are a blessing and it has been a privilege to watch you birth your dream. Chip McGregor, David Garfinkle, and all those who make it all come together, you are appreciated.

About the Authors

HOLLY VIRDEN, who founded Segue Media, a Christian-driven public relations and promotional company in Nashville, has worked and traveled with many high-profile Christian artists including Kim Hill, Sierra, and Bob Carlisle, as well as record labels such as Star Song, Forefront, Pamplin, and Sparrow. She has worked behind the scenes for such conferences as Women of Faith, Women of Virtue, Focus on the Family, and Moody's Conferences for Women.

MICHELLE MCKINNEY HAMMOND is the author of eighteen books, including *What to Do Until Love Finds You.* She is also a cohost of the regionally broadcast, Emmy-nominated television show *Aspiring Women.* As founder of HeartWing Ministries, Michelle has been a sought-after speaker for women's conferences, retreats, and seminars including Women of Virtue, Focus on the Family, and Moody's Conferences for Women. She has been featured on the cover of numerous publications and on television programs including *Politically Incorrect,* BET's *OH Drama,* and NBC's *The Other Half.*